ON THE NATURE OF VALUE

The Philosophy of Samuel Alexander

ON THE
NATURE OF VALUE

The Philosophy of Samuel Alexander

MILTON R. KONVITZ

MORNINGSIDE HEIGHTS · NEW YORK

KING'S CROWN PRESS

1946

Reprinted with the permission of Milton R. Konvitz

JOHNSON REPRINT CORPORATION
111 Fifth Avenue, New York, N.Y. 10003

JOHNSON REPRINT COMPANY LTD.
Berkeley Square House, London, W. 1

For

FRANK H. SOMMER

GEORGE H. SABINE

"Friendship is a sheltering tree"

Professor S. Alexander's contribution to the theory of value—in his monumental *Space, Time, and Deity*, as well as in *Beauty and Other Forms of Value*, in his *Philosophical and Literary Pieces*, and other writings—is a notable one, worthy of much study and discussion. In this book we propose to analyze his views, consider them from the perspective of the history of philosophy, and provide a criticism from the standpoint of our own views as to the nature of value. Our chief interest is not Alexander but the nature of value; hence the title: *On the Nature of Value: the Philosophy of Samuel Alexander*.

I am happy to have the opportunity to mention with gratitude the names of friends who have, in one way or another, made a contribution to this volume: Dean G. Watts Cunningham, Cornell University; Professor William Curtis Swabey, New York University; Professor Herbert W. Schneider, Columbia University; Dr. Rubin Gotesky; and Professor Henry Alonzo Myers, Cornell University.

I am grateful, too, to The Macmillan Company, for kind permission to quote from the works of Alexander; the editors of the *Journal of Philosophy*, for permission to reprint Chapter VII; the editors of *Ethics*, for permission to reprint Chapter VI; and Mr. Henry M. Silver, 2nd, manager of King's Crown Press. I wish to thank also Mr. E. R. B. Willis, associate librarian of Cornell University, for courtesies over a period of many years.

Finally, my gratitude to my wife, for encouragement and forbearance, acts of commission and omission.

M. R. K.

Contents

*I*T WILL be seen that the first three chapters stand somewhat apart from the rest of the essay. In them the attempt is made to convey the spirit and logic of Professor S. Alexander's enquiry, mainly by direct reference to his works and partly by contrast with the views of others.

While the problems therein treated are, we think, interesting on their own account, their solution, we fear, does not shed much, if any, light on a consideration of the difficulties involved in the treatment of any one of the particular values. The whole discussion in these several chapters serves, perhaps, as a metaphysic of value, and so supplies no content to the form of any one value. We fail to see, e.g., how the notion of adaptation, imported by Alexander from the science of biology, and asserted by him to be a character of value in general, really helps him, or can be of any help to any-one, in a treatment of beauty or truth; and, indeed, when he comes to consider these special values, he seems to forget the notion en-tirely. The discussion, then, in the first three chapters tends to set the mind rather than fill it.

We wish to be clear on this point: that we do not speak for our-selves in these chapters, howsoever warmly we may seem to be defending Alexander's position. We only attempt to place his doc-trine in as favorable a light as possible. Also: the fact that these chapters do not seem to have great pertinence to what follows them, is a failure which we beg the reader not to charge to us. We like to think that there is a close bond between metaphysics and a theory of value; but in the case of Alexander we have difficulty in seeing what that bond is. E.g., when we come to a consideration of the problem of truth, it will be seen that our sharp criticism of

Alexander's conclusions on this head is based on his failure to remember the logic of his metaphysic when treating of this special subject. But, since our subject is chiefly Alexander's theory, we cannot omit an analysis of a phase of the subject to which he himself devotes considerable attention.

When we come to treat of each of the values separately, it will be seen that the central notion in each instance is coherence. Alexander defines truth as coherence; so, too, goodness. In the case of beauty, while he says that "the beauty of the beautiful object lies in the congruence or coherence of its parts," [1] he does not again use the term, and in his many articles and addresses he speaks only of the form of a work of art. He does not define form, but he may mean the coherence of its parts.

Our critique will show that coherence in goodness and truth, and form in art, while of the utmost significance, do not exhaust the nature of the values. In order to do this, we are necessitated into an analysis of the nature of meaning. The fourth chapter, then, on "Meaning and Value," is transitional, and introduces the chapters that follow. In the chapter on beauty it will be seen that the meaning of a work of art is wider or more than its form; in the chapter on goodness, that while coherence is a necessary character of morality, it is not the sufficient character; and in the chapter on truth, that meaning is wider than existence, that there may be said to be two tests of truth, depending on whether the meanings are ontological or deontological in intent. [2]

Our approach, then, is not through coherence, and our main line

1. *Space, Time, and Deity*, II, 293.
Professor Alexander's treatment of value is in the second volume, Book III, chapter 9, of *Space, Time, and Deity*. References to pages in this volume, and in periodicals and other of his works, are given always when passages are quoted, and not infrequently when an important passage is paraphrased.
While some of Alexander's articles have been incorporated in the book *Beauty and other Forms of Value*, references are to the original articles, for I agree with John Laird that "the earlier essays, although (or perhaps because) they 'plunged' so provocatively, are severally more adequate than the later and smoother narrative." Memoir by Laird in Alexander, S., *Philosophical and Literary Pieces*, 85–86.
2. We prefer to say a test of truth and a test of validity. See *post* Chapter 7 and Conclusion.

of criticism of Alexander is that he is obsessed with the notion of coherence, and so falls into the error of defining all of the "tertiary qualities" in terms of that notion exclusively. The emphasis we place on systematic meaning in Chapter 4 does not preëmpt us from an adverse criticism of Alexander, for we do not pretend that the discovery of a type of meaning, howsoever important, by itself exhausts the nature of meaning.

The order in which the particular values are herein treated is not the same as that followed by Alexander. His order of presentation is as follows: truth, goodness, beauty. It may be that his order prejudiced his mind, so that after treating of the logical coherence of judgments or propositions he was ready to find the coherence of wills as the essence of morality. At any rate, we prefer not to follow his sequence, primarily for the reason that the aesthetic problem permits of a freer treatment of the nature of meaning than do the other values. Truth is considered last for the reason that the consideration necessitates a collection of the various strands and shreds of theory that we develop by preference in the earlier chapters.

It remains to be noted here that we do not undertake anywhere in the essay to define the meaning of coherence *by that name.* We trust that our analysis of systematic meaning in Chapter 4 will be considered adequate for all purposes. We may add that Alexander himself does not attempt a definition. Having as a model Bradley's attempt in the *Essays on Truth and Reality,*[3] his failure seems almost inexcusable. It, therefore, remains open to free speculation whether or no Alexander would accept Bradley's definition of coherence as a system of knowledge having as its inseparable characters consistency and comprehensiveness.

As this Introduction forecasts, it will be soon discovered that the critic and Professor Alexander are not in agreement on all vital issues. But we frankly say that we know of no contemporary philosopher who, more than he, merits close study and respectful audience; and it is, really, only with much timidity and humbleness that one ventures to differ with him.

3. Pp. 202, 210, 223.

Metaphysics and Value

I. DISVALUE OF VALUE

*W*E ARE ACQUAINTED with the attempt made by Mr. Joseph Wood Krutch to disvalue values. With the pathos of one who lives on locusts and wild honey, he cries that the world has suddenly become empty of all truth, goodness, beauty. That which to our fathers was so variously lovely and good, is to the sons and daughters a place of darkness, inhabited by creatures who, in Carlyle's epithet, are barely more than featherless bipeds; men who claim no glorious heritage and foresee no splendid destiny; too puny on life's stage to be taken for tragic heroes, too honest to pretend to be heroic tragedians; tender in their copulations, but never knowing chivalry in love; only remembering, what their fathers have told them, that once upon a time, even when they went in to the daughters of men, human beings thought they were the sons of God; faintly and sadly recalling that their mothers would put them to sleep with bewitching tales of One called God, but who, they now know better (since the descent from the mountain of Nietzsche's Zarathustra), is as dead as the squirrel that gathered nuts in the woods some score years ago. It is the philosophy of the New Enlightenment; the philosophy of despair, frustration. We are the characters who talk their way through Aldous Huxley's early novels, living a life without significance, without love, believing nothing, caring for nothing, sick in the pit of the belly to the very death; each of us, in the words of T. S. Eliot, "an old man in a dry month," muttering incoherencies,

I grow old . . . I grow old . . .
I shall wear the bottoms of my trousers rolled

lost in aimless revery, hearing always the wind making mournful sound and the waters beating on the beach, saying to ourselves, we are the hollow men, we are the stuffed men, our heads are filled with straw, our voices dry; to those already in death's kingdom, we are not even lost violent souls, but only creatures who inhabit a dead land, a waste land, a cactus land, empty men hoping for a twilight death that will not mean new life but extinction; hollow men, stuffed men.

This *tedium vitae,* that characterizes much of contemporary life and letters, has its roots in a dry, rocky, pest-ridden soil. Take away his rattle from an infant and he cries as though something cosmically catastrophic has happened, and his heart would burst asunder because of his grief and sense of loss, emptiness, frustration. They had walked with scales over their eyes, seeing nothing, fancying the heart's desire, building altars, in their blind, staggering way, to unhuman gods, who, they liked to think, made up the choir of heaven and the furniture of earth. A little evolution, Marxism, relativity and the higher criticism, and all is ashes and dustheap, and the votaries are stricken, like the youth in Schiller's poem who dared lift the veil of truth. Not much more has been disclosed to us than our fathers knew. Our knowledge is still only a dim torch that lights our path barely a step ahead. But there are some things we no longer believe in, and, to one who values truth, the elimination of an error is prized nearly as much as a new revelation. Man is an animal that will not, like the dog, go back to his vomit; no matter how slightly we may have lifted the veil, no Agamemnon today will sacrifice his Iphigenia on a religious altar to appease a blood-thirsty god. We will make new blunders, but we will not, once we discover their nature, repeat old ones. The younger Eliot and Krutch, and others of their like, find themselves without a mythology. God's no longer in his heaven; therefore, all's wrong with the world. God was the elephant on whom the world rested; remove the support, and the superstructure totters and falls. If God is not on his throne in the heavenly palace, surrounded by the cherubim and seraphim and the holy chayoth, ever watchful that Justice shall not slumber nor Mercy sleep, nor redeemed man be replaced by the sun as the center and cynosure of all things,—then things do not hang together, the world is one large madhouse, and there is nothing to do and nothing to think, only to let one's brain tick-tock, tick-tock, until merciful death will still it. It is a sad tale indeed, worthy of another Jeremiad; for the temple is laid waste, the money-changers have been chased, the guardians of the faith and the money exchange are without dignity, pride has left the earth, chivalry (the pretense of condescension and the cloak of contempt) is dead. There are no more anointed among us, none who can live as the lily of the field, neither toiling nor spinning; men are without leisure, without amenities, without grand gestures; it is so dreary, death has invaded life, there is nothing for us to do but to go to sleep, let the stream of consciousness, like a river, run its course without impediment. It is a sad tale, indeed, and told by an idiot. The solution lies in Art as an Ivory Tower, and *as a way of escape,* an aristocratic distraction; the brain fancying plots in which the boy always gets the girl, and the fancied world is a Garden of Epicurus; a tale signifying nothing.

II. VALUE-CENTRIC UNIVERSE

That is one way of looking at it, the way of despair. There are others who, too, have seen the writing on the wall, but who will not put on sack-cloth and strew ashes on their heads. Some men have no memories and no hopes; because they do not know how to issue their strength, they feel frustrated. Other men are die-hards. They hold life more dearly because of their fond recollections and their midday dreams. Such are found at the tail-end of every losing army. They do not think of victory; but pray for a miracle or hope for a truce.

Professor Urban is aware that the attempt has been made to find for values a local habitation among the natural objects that people the universe, facts among other facts, like eating, perception of color, sexual reproduction, respiration. But this involves another Copernican revolution, and that is unthinkable. The sun may have displaced the earth as the universal fulcrum, but that was a change only in astronomical charts. In philosophy, not only is the earth still the center, but man is, in another sense, the center of the earth: the point about which all things and influences concentrate and from which they proceed; and the central fact in human existence is value. Hence, value is the central fact in the universe.

Urban avers that he belongs to the Great Tradition in philosophy, that he speaks "the perennial truths of traditional thought." He finds the world ultimately meaningful and intelligible; intelligible, that is, in some sense "beyond" the sensible and phenomenal. That value and reality are ultimately inseparable, he takes as axiomatic. The problems of value are central, and it is no longer possible merely to write a chapter on value at the end of a philosophical treatise.

He rejects the hedonistic explanation. Why should pleasure confer a value? he asks. In all such explanations valuableness is already assumed as an intrinsic quality of pleasure or of fulfillment. The real question is this: Is the interest itself worthy of being satisfied? Is the object worthy of being of interest?

Nor can value be deduced from concepts of adaptation, for all such deductions are circular. Adaptation involves end or purpose, and end or purpose presupposes value. Also the idea of degrees of value as linked with development involves this difficulty; for if it be maintained that the better is the more highly developed, then development is necessarily improvement, and the notion of improvement involves value.

Value is a logically primitive concept, like existence and being, though even the latter two are reducible to value. The judgment of value involves an existential judgment, but it is more than a judgment of existence together with a feeling; for value is not a quality. It is an objective, and exemplifies a unique form of objectivity. Valuation is noetic, yet value is not a quality perceived or intuited, but rather a form of objectivity acknowledged. Value does not exist or subsist: its being is its validity. All cognition is valuational, and truth and reality are values to be acknowledged rather than existents or subsistents to be apprehended. Value, he reiterates, neither exists nor subsists; it is "simply" valid. It is the very essence

8 *On the Nature of Value*

of reality; the very substance and essence of a thing. He quotes
Lotze approvingly, that an ought sets the play of thoughts, of
ground, cause, purpose, in movement. And he quotes from Witt-
genstein, that "The solution of the riddle of life in space and time
lies outside space and time," and from Aristotle, that fire or earth
or any such element is not the reason why things manifest goodness and beauty. Space and time are phenomenal of a non-spatial
and non-temporal order of meanings and values; [1] but he asserts
that "the inalienable difference" between what is and what ought
to be, between existence and value, is "the ultimate mystery." [2]

As the doctrine is formulated by Urban, it is not only a mystery,
but a metaphysical obscurity. Our present concern is not with the
minutiae of Urban's statement. Regarding his argument as to
adaptation, e.g., it might be said simply with Lamarck that adaptation to environment means only an equilibration of forces or
energies, the adjustment of the energies of living beings to the
energies of the environment; or with Darwin, that adaptation is to
be explained by accidental variations which, if suitable to the environment, are perpetuated by inheritance, the phenomenon involving no concept of end or purpose, or value. "Good" means
"able to survive"; "better" means "better fitted to survive." [3]

What is more important, however, is that this traditional view of
value is a sterile virgin. It is Münsterberg's Overself, the Metaphysical Absolute Will. It is a theological doctrine; it requires a
view of the earth as anthropocentric, and the universe as geocentric
and value-centric.[4] It is a "reduction" of realty to the scale of the
infinite. And what can we do with it? You cannot bake bread by
it, nor order a community, nor inspire the musician or painter;
values are absolute, occult, arbitrary. Above all, the doctrine is
words we do not really understand. It is astounding that in this late
day one needs to deny that man is the center of all things and that
everything revolves about the puny planet called the earth. Ur-

1. *The Intelligible World*, p. 268. See also Preface, and pp. 129, 133, 136,
162, 232, 273.
2. *Ibid.*, p. 247.
3. Cf. G. E. Moore, *Philosophical Studies*, "Conception of Intrinsic Value,"
p. 256; Parker, *Human Values*, "Value and Reason," p. 109.
4. Cf. Moore, *op. cit.*, p. 259.

ban's answer to the query, What is value? recalls to mind Spengler's judgment on the question, What is time? No one, he said, should ever have been allowed to ask such a question.

We shall have occasion to recur to a consideration of the Value-centric Predicament, particularly to what extent it is involved in the view that value is a fact, and that value may be found on levels of existence lower than the conscious. Enough has been said, we trust, to prepare us for a treatment of these problems; and also for a contrast with the spirit of Alexander's enquiry.

III. NATURE AND VALUE

Where others find despair or the occasion for escape, Professor Alexander finds delight. Man is not outside of nature but in it, like the ant and the beaver and the eagle. The universe is a spatio-temporal system, a coherent whole, internally consistent, intelligible, and, on certain levels,[5] possessing value. Traditional philosophy followed this path of procedure: it assumed a theory of value and from it eked out a metaphysic. The scholastic's *ens realissimum* and Plato's Form of Good allowed no distinction between *essentia* and *esse*, value and existence. The supreme value is also the source of all existence. It was the sacerdotal view of the universe. Alexander, on the contrary, is a profane philosopher. "We humans," he says, "who live at the level of the sixth day of creation, are so unwilling to go back to the fourth day when there were no animals to see and hear."[6] He is super-Copernican, for he is not content to deny only that the world is the center of the universe; he also denies that man is the center of the world. He is also super-Darwinian; for to him man is not the ultimate aim of nature.

Alexander's temper is to de-anthropomorphize; to order man and mind to their proper place among the world of finite things. As a realist or naturalist he seeks, on the one hand, to divest physical things of the coloring which they have received from the vanity or arrogance of mind; on the other, to assign them, along with

5. Cf. *Space, Time, and Deity*, II, 302: "value . . . *perhaps* is a common feature of all existents"; p. 410: "and values are evolved within the level of mind, and indeed with proper qualifications within *every* level." (Italics supplied.)

6. *Basis of Realism*, p. 25.

minds, their due measure of self-existence.[7] His naturalism is not
the mere habit of finding a place for man and his interests in a
scheme of things which includes and starts with physical nature.
That method, he says, is common to all honest philosophy. The
distinctive feature of naturalism is to be found in the belief that
the physical aspect of things is pervasive, or that on one side of
them they are all natural or even mechanical.[8]

From this viewpoint, value also must be accounted for upon a
naturalistic basis. One ought not to fear, with the counsellors of
despair, of whom we treated at the outset, that an understanding of
their *modus operandi,* or the discovery of their physical foundation, will destroy the practically good, the genuinely and verifiably
true, and the aesthetically beautiful. The naturalist does not come
to destroy or to fulfill, but only to understand. It is to be conceded,
however, that with understanding does come destruction and fulfillment—that is inevitable,—the destruction of occult powers and
faculties and qualities; the fulfillment of what is in the capacity of
men to fulfill, the earthly, the human. Naturalism does not imply
the artificiality of value. Right and wrong are man-made, but they
are not, for that reason, simply conventional or artificial. "Right
represents human nature at its best," [9] and what is best, as what is
true, is the discovery not of unaided intuition or reason, but of
experiment; "it is an expedient struck out in the effort to maximise
satisfactions." [10]

To maintain that the human values are not isolated or exceptional
things, but are specimens of something more general, of which we
shall treat subsequently, is not to debase them in any way, no
more than it is to debase knowing when it is considered as merely
one illustration of the relations between finites.[11] Alexander ad-
monishes that he who fancies that the community of our values
with values on lower levels of existence destroys the sacredness of
truth or goodness or beauty, "forgets that to describe correctly
does not alter the reality described." [12] In a passage which contrasts
with Plato's remark in the *Euthyphro* that the holy is loved because

7. *Ibid.,* p. 1.   8. *Chronicon Spinozanum,* 1927, p. 14.
9. *Ibid.,* p. 23.   10. *Ibid.,* p. 24.
11. *Space, Time, and Deity,* II, 229.   12. *Ibid.,* p. 313.

it is holy, and it is not holy because it is loved, Alexander says that the preciousness of values consists in their being values. "On the contrary, the human values by being thus related to other values do not lose their preciousness, but in fact preserve it by forfeiting their mystery. Human nature does not lose by becoming intelligible but comes into its own." [13]

He protests against the philosophical method which adopts human value, because it is the tensest of our experiences about finite things, as the clue to the nature of reality. For practice, the values are precious, but they are not therefore more real than other realities. To start with the unanalyzed conception of value, and measure reality by it, "is to erect what weighs most in our human existence into the exemplar of realty, and to assign to value blindly a function which it cannot perform. It discolors the truth with our affections, and it interferes with what Goethe described as our business in acquiring knowledge, of laying our minds alongside things." [14]

Bosanquet, in his Adamson lecture on the *Distinction between Mind and Its Objects*, says that the underlying motive in subjective idealism is a recognition of the necessity that the most interesting things should have at least as much reality as anything else, and that mind should not be cut off from its objects, which constitute nature and the world.[15] Alexander undoubtedly shares this sentiment. In his attempt, as a realist, to avoid psycho-mania, he does not become a victim to psycho-phobia.[16] He is not afraid to recognize the reality of mind and its acts in a surrounding world of non-mental reals; and among mind's products are values.

By way of anticipation it may be said that on the question of the nature of the reality of values, Alexander and Bosanquet, though widely differing on other questions, are in substantial agreement. Both maintain that the relation involved in the value situation is not of subject on one side and object on the other. Subject-object in unlinkable union is the basic value-fact. There are no sides, except for purposes of philosophical analysis. For the value situation, subject, mind, consciousness, or life is an envelop-

13. *Ibid.,* II, 314.   14. *Ibid.*   15. P. 10.
16. Cf. Clarke, *A Study in the Logic of Value*, p. 118.

ing atmosphere, whose nature is to include. It is a world, not an object in a world; in nature and intent, it is a whole, while the object is a fragment. While with regard to lower metaphysical levels, we cannot, with some idealists, say that only the whole is real; with regard to value, this is the only position.[17]

IV. DEITY AND VALUE

Professor Mackenzie, while accepting the evolutionary postulate, and affirming that mind may be the result of material circumstances, believes that mind may be the explanation of the process out of which it has grown.[18] Considered as the expression of a wish, we might be sympathetic; as an argument, however, it is an instance of the fallacy *hysteron proteron*, the attempt to explain first things by last things. Feuerbach's statement is well known, that backwards he is in accord with the materialists, but not forwards. Professor Mackenzie is on the same road, but, when he reaches his destination and retraces his steps in imagination, he remarks that this is the last for which the first was made. It is almost a pathetic spectacle, man frantically clutching at a straw and crying, "You will save me! You must save me!" The theological explanation of cosmic and human phenomena—why the stars are lit in the heavens and why man, whimpering and suffering, goes up and down on the face of the earth—may be difficult to profess publicly; though Maritain and Massis, T. S. Eliot, Chesterton, and Belloc have braved the censure. Professor Mackenzie's method is a more subtle one; it is the attempt to achieve in philosophy what is impossible in dietetics; that is, to eat his cake and have it. He admits all the premises and data of the naturalist, until he himself is pointed to as a specimen; and then, like the little boy who had quarreled, he "takes it *all* back," and says he did not mean what he said. I cannot suppress the feeling that there is something of self-deception in this procedure; like Browning writing "Rabbi Ben Ezra," of old age as the best in man's life, while in his heart of hearts he must have known that youth is like summer morn and summer brave, and old age is full of care and winter weather.

17. Cf. Bosanquet, *op. cit.*, pp. 27-8.
18. *Fundamental Problems of Life*, p. 47.

Now, Alexander, it seems, on the one hand agrees with Feuerbach. God, he thinks, is the universe as possessing deity. Deity belongs to the order of perfection, rather than value.[19] It is the next higher empirical quality than mind.[20]

But, on the other hand, he seems to go all the way with Mackenzie, and hold that while deity may, so to speak, grow out of the universe, it is also the explanation of the process out of which it grows. Deity, he says, is "in the line of mental values and grows out of them." In the wider sense of value—"the return of the isolated finite into communion with reality"—deity "remains next to mental and even human values, but it is also in the line of all value, and our values are but its proximate material. In this sense," he continues, "deity represents the conservation of all values or valuable existence whatever, and is an outgrowth from them. All values are conserved in God's deity." [21]

The difference between Alexander and Mackenzie is that to the former deity is not yet an actuality. We sense deity in our feeling of going out towards the world in a quality higher than that of mind or any of the human values.[22] Deity is not realized but prognosticated. For this reason, it is not imperative that Alexander's naturalism be looked upon as compromised or deserted. For as soon as he takes wing and seems bent on leaving the precincts of the universe, he ceases his metaphysical function, and we need not follow him. On parting from him, we could say, with the poet, that at least the past is with us.

We would rather, of course, that a naturalistic philosopher would not indulge in speculation as to what will be in the latter end of days. But there is no law against such speculation. Such an activity, however, and its results, so far as metaphysics is concerned, are altogether gratuitous. The philosopher's task is to schematize the universe as he finds it, and not to prophesy.

Alexander finds the universe big with deity. It may be that we live in an expanding universe and that it is pregnant with something or other. But no philosopher ought to stake his professional reputation on the prognostication that the offspring will be deity

19. *Space, Time, and Deity*, II, 410.   20. *Ibid.*, p. 345.
21. *Ibid.*, p. 416.   22. *Ibid.*, p. 408.

or devil. To Alexander the birth of deity must be literally and metaphorically an act of God—and it is only decent that the courtesy we show a daughter of man, when we draw the veil of secrecy about her, be accorded in this transaction to God himself.

V. VALUATION OF VALUE

Contrary to the traditional philosophies generally, in Alexander's metaphysical scheme value does occupy only a single chapter towards the end of the book. After treating of the universe as a spatio-temporal whole, characterized by certain categories and qualities, among the latter being mind and its acts, he concerns himself with value. This procedure is of great significance. Metaphysics must have room for value, no less than for physical bodies and mental phenomena. There is value in the universe, as well as cats and dogs and mice; but it is only a natural phenomenon, like them; only a fact among a multitude of other facts. Alexander's system is probably the first in which value is located in so humble a metaphysical place; among the lowly objects of experience, it is neither deacon nor sexton, but one in an equal democracy.

This putting value in its proper place does not imply that value is itself evaluated. For a naturalistic metaphysic value is a *fact*—not an *instrument;* something to be investigated, not used. It is only the ought of scientific logic that directs the philosopher to treat of the subject of value only after he has first dealt with Space-Time, the categories, qualities, and mind; not greatly different from the ought of the gastronomic logic that directs us to eat anchovies as an appetizer rather than as a dessert.

Even were we to admit that Alexander's scheme of presentation does implicitly involve an evaluation of value, it will not therefore mean that a stone has been removed from the foundation of his structure. If the philosophers make their universe value-centric, does it not imply that they have evaluated value as worthy of the place of honor? Then surely they cannot object to another evaluating value otherwise?

But the concession need not be taken to mean that Alexander, too, is value-centric. Millions of citizens may vote and elect one of their own to the presidency. Thereafter they are governed in part by the man whom they themselves have chosen. To a Martian, or a dull monarchist of England of pre-Commonwealth times, this might sound like a strange paradox. Value may be like the law-abiding citizen in a republic. The vote is his, but he knows that he is not wise or good enough to hold first place; so he elects another. There is nothing strange in value knowing its place in the scheme of things, though it, itself, schematizes the things; just as there is nothing strange in a man knowing his place in society, though it is society, of which he is a free member, that places him.

CHAPTER 2

General Theory of Value

I. VALUE AND FACT

*A*s FAR BACK as 1892 Alexander was concerned with the idea of value. In an article in *Mind* [1] he undertook an analysis of the concept, and the results therein stated, except for changes in some details, he maintained thereafter.

He begins by making the commonplace distinction between judgments that are in intent factual and those that are normative. Of the latter species of judgments, there are those which express scientific truth, or moral goodness, or aesthetic beauty. Normative judgments do not merely assert a finding, as when we say, "This is a house"; there is something more; they imply that something has been put on its trial and judged. When we say, "It is *true*, this *is* a house," it is obvious that something has happened to the former proposition; it has been weighed and found not wanting.

This would seem to lead to the inference that there is an irreducible difference between facts and value; something we have been prepared to deny by our preliminary statements. But Alexander does not draw this inference, though he is not unaware that he must speak very guardedly here.

There is a distinction between fact and value, but it is not an ultimate one. Values are derived from the commonest facts of human life. To be led to make an unbridgeable chasm between existence and value, one must be guilty of the confusion of the

1. 17 N.S., 31, 1892.

practically invaluable with the theoretically unique. Many of us are, in social morals, conventional; not desirous of seeing radical changes instituted. This may be due to our habits, or a happy marriage, or a financial investment. But we must not presume, because we take our interests so seriously, to view that which we link intimately with our heart's desire as being, therefore, something in its essence unique, irreducible, beyond the pale of workaday things; mayhap having a functional relevance to the facts of existence, but not an essential connection therewith.

On the contrary, Alexander maintains that value is only a particular kind of fact; admittedly, a fact of a higher, more complex order; but essentially a thing natural, and in direct continuity with all other facts.

II. PRINCIPLE OF NATURAL ELECTION

Consideration of value as fact suggests a comparison of Alexander's view with Laird's principle of natural election.[2] A discussion of the principle will serve also to introduce Alexander's notion of levels of value.

The principle of natural election may also be called the principle of non-indifference in nature, or natural-election-or-rejection. It is observable in non-conscious as well as in conscious beings, or, stating it more correctly, the principle is found in conscious as well as in non-conscious beings. It exemplifies the question, as it were, that natural objects ask, "*Quid interfuit?*"—What did it matter? Selection is the essence of non-indifference; that is, acceptance or rejection. But this is not to attribute an occult hidden will to every object, resulting in a panpsychical metaphysic. On the contrary, it may lead one to seek the springs of conscious will in non-conscious matter. Selection is not peculiarly psychological, for it is more extensive than life or consciousness.

The principle is relevant to a theory of value, for it suggests that value is merely whatever matters to or concerns a thing. Value is thus factual and objective, "for things *are* in the relation in question." [3]

2. *The Idea of Value*, chs. 3 and 9.
3. *Ibid.*, 305.

But a *caveat* must be entered, else the doctrine is open to serious misunderstanding. The principle of natural election and value are not identical. The latter is only a species. Conscious choice, Laird admits, is *not* the same as unconscious natural election.[4]

Recognition of the connection between value and natural election, the former being the human manifestation of the latter general principle, has a three-fold significance: (1) it leads one to conclude that consciousness is not the *differentia* in terms of which value is to be defined, for other than the human animal manifests both selection and consciousness; (2) that value is not dependent on cognition, for men prize what they need, what will make a difference to them, and yet they may not know what they need;[5] (3) that value is a natural fact.

Each of the conclusions is of great importance and is in turn suggestive of implications, but in the present connection our concern is only with the third, because it leads to the question which our discussion suggests; namely, if value is a natural fact, and has its affinities with all other facts of existence, does it not mean that all the universe is characterized by value, and is, perhaps, value-centric? This question is obviously distinguishable from our earlier one, in which we considered the inference that the universe is value-centric if value is found as a fact in a universe which consists in the main of things which have not the character of value; that is, if our judgment that the universe is a spatio-temporal whole, which admits in some of its parts of the character of value, does not imply that value is the central fact in the universe.

It seems that the present question raises a difficulty which is verbal, and indicates that it were best for metaphysics generally not to use a term like value, which, because of its vagueness and its rich store of implicated transcendentals and spiritualities, leads to a multitude of problems for every solution it suggests.

But first let us indicate that the question issues out of a logical fallacy; namely, the converse fallacy of accident, *a dicto secundum*

---

4. P. 101.

5. This is, too, Meinong's position, that value is founded in feeling rather than desire, for we value things we do not desire, and we value what we no longer seek. *Zur Grundlegung der allgemeine Wert-Theorie*, pp. 37–45.

quid ad dictum simpliciter, which consists in arguing that what is true of a thing under a named condition, can be asserted of it simply or in its essential nature, or that what is true only when certain conditions are present, is true generally. Parts of the universe under certain conditions have the character of value. This does not logically imply that all the universe, and under all conditions, has that character, or that in its very essence it is value. It is to be noted that it is only a metaphysical bias which denies the reality of parts as such that can be led easily to fall into this fallacy.

Reverting to the verbal difficulty, we dare say that if we forget value, substitute for it natural election or some other convenient phrase, there will be nothing to arouse excitement even in the most inflammable metaphysician. He would simply proceed to ask, first, what is natural election in so far as its various kinds agree? and secondly, what different kinds of natural election are there? The other questions which use of the term value almost demands, will not even suggest themselves; e.g., is the difference between natural election and other facts ultimate? or is natural election the very essence of the universe? the ground, cause, and purpose of all things? At the most, he might be tempted to make of it something like Schopenhauer's Will; but then he will view it as something tangible, flowing, as that which is manifested in a falling rock, a dog on a blood scent, and a man in love; nothing attenuated, nor everywhere implying mind.

III. ADAPTATION AND LEVELS OF VALUE

In *Space, Time, and Deity* we get a more analytic discussion of value than in Alexander's early article in *Mind,* but, as we have said, the doctrine underwent no important change during the many intervening years.

Truth, goodness, and beauty are named tertiary qualities, and though it is they which in the strict sense have the right to the name value, they are not the only kind of values. Value in a more extended sense reaches lower down than man, "and perhaps is a common feature of all finites." [6] Value does not begin at the human level. Wider than, e.g., moral goodness and badness, are goodness

6. *Space, Time, and Deity,* II, 302.

and badness in things, and good and evil in the objects which satisfy them. The values strictly so-called, the tertiary qualities, are but the highest instance of a feature of things which extends over a much wider range, and is found in the nature of Space-Time itself; "and may even be empirically universal." [7]

What is that feature of things, founded in the nature of Space-Time itself, which is value in its variety of levels and manifestations? That feature is adaptation. On the level of life value exists as the persistence of adapted forms of living beings. To a type that has adapted itself, that part of its environment on which it can react so as to sustain its life has value for the type, and the typical individual is the subject of value or is a valuable form of life. Those individuals or types which, in their relation to the environment, fail in competition with the values, are the unvalues and are eliminated. These include both the unsuccessful types, and the individuals of the successful type which vary too far from the standard and are thus incompatible with the type.

The essential marks of value which we will find exhibited in the tertiary qualities appear, on the level of existence, in the form suitable thereto. The intrinsic features of value do not vary, but only the subjects of valuation, and with them their objects, which differ at different levels of development in Space-Time. In all cases value resides in the compound of the subject with its object. Thus, a creature has value under one environment, and none or less in other surroundings.

This suggests that permanence of the valuable type is secured by the process of rivalry, by which the failures are excluded. Darwinism or natural selection, Alexander says in an address on Spinoza, is the natural history of value. [8] This position he maintains also in *Space, Time, and Deity*. [9] Darwinism is the history of how values come into existence in the sphere of life.

Natural selection has been thought to be indifferent to value, for the reason that it has been misunderstood as an explanation of how types are generated, or as the actual cause of successful types. The misconception is that the fittest is what survives, and so we

7. *Ibid.*, 311.   8. *Chronicon Spinozanum*, 1927, p. 24.
9. II, 309.

get only the tautology of the survival of the fittest, or the survival of that which survives. To identify value with fitness is to add nothing but a new term, not a new conception. The correct view is that the survival in question is that of the most favored types. The cause of success is not natural selection but the qualities of the types engaged in the competition. The struggle is only the process whereby their qualities or virtues or gifts receive expression. Thus, to illustrate by an example, the cause of a successful issue in a war is not the fighting, but the character and resources of the combatants. Natural selection is therefore wholly concerned with value. It means that values emerge through the trial of various types under certain external conditions. Natural selection is thus wholly conversant with value; it is the means to the supremacy of the adapted over the unadapted types; and thus by the rejection of unvalue, value is brought into being, or, as Alexander says, value emerges.

Thus, on the level of life, value in the organism belongs not to the organism in itself, but to the organism in its relation to its environment, the conditions of life; and so, a type which can live and function successfully under certain conditions, may be unsuited to a set of different circumstances, and so be a value in one relation and an unvalue in another. The doctrine of natural selection, then, supplies us the natural history of values in the world of life. We shall see that it supplies equally that history in the world of mind; but first let us consider its possible application in the sphere of existence below life.

Alexander admits that at present it is clearly a matter of speculation how far downwards below the level of life "the principle of adaptation or valuation" extends.[10] He suggests that the chemical elements and the permanent forces of energy are the outcome of a process of adaptation. This should not shock; for in their simplest expression values imply only adaptation, which applies to any finite complex of space-time; they do not imply anything which depends on the quality of life or consciousness in the subject of value. Space-Time is broken up into volumes of space-time, which are things, relatively independent, each with a certain internal and

10. II, 310.

external configuration. "Adaptation is the return of these complexes out of separation from the whole into unity with it." [11] Of course, point-instants which have no complexity of structure are always adapted to their surroundings. But the complex combinations of them may be inconformable to the other complexes to which they respond and in thus responding maintain themselves; this is obvious in the instance of living and higher forms. "The competition of the reals which are composites of things and their environment is the settling down of this variety into stability." [12] Man alone experiments consciously, but it is not he alone who experiments. Besides conscious experimentation, there are many simpler grades, such as trial and error, by which living types are able to vary within limits without suffering destruction; the simple process of the destruction of the unfit; and perhaps there is a simpler process still.

To suppose that the process of adaptation begins with living forms is to imply that the empirical things on the lower levels are so simple in structure that they do not come into competition with one another; but what evidence is available seems to indicate that the process is one that is universally prevalent.

In brief, then, value depends on adaptation, and adaptation is an *a priori* character of empirical existence, the return of complex configurations of space-time from isolation into relation with the rest of Space-Time, and the process assumes the character of value through the rejection of the unadapted unvalues.[13] Value may be called a derivative universal character. It is not a primary categorial character, for it presupposes the existence of things as empirical or as possessing quality; and it is not an empirical character, for it arises out of the participation of things in Space-Time. Every finite is a part of Space-Time, and is accommodated or adapted to its surroundings in it, thus participating in the whole. Human values, or the tertiary qualities, are founded on the adaptation of mind to other minds and to the world of other things. When there is a failure of adaptation, the unvalues—error, badness, ugliness—arise.[14]

11. II, 311.　　　12. *Ibid.*　　　13. II, 312.　　　14. II, 78–79.

CHAPTER 3

Man and Value

I. VALUE AS A SUBJECT-OBJECT RELATION

*I*N ALL VALUE, on whatever level found, there are two sides; namely, the subject of valuation and the object of value, "and the value resides in the relation between the two"; [1] that is to say, the value does not exist in either apart from the other. There is value in the object only as possessed by the subject, and there is value in the subject only as possessing the object. When a subject is in relation to an object, it values that object, attributes value to it, but the attribution of value to either member can take place only when there is the combination of subject and object. Value, Alexander seems to hold, belongs to the compound of subject and object, and values, as truths, moral goods, works of beauty, or the true thinker, the good man, the man of aesthetic sensibility, are valuable derivatively from the compound.[2] Strictly speaking, there are values only in respect of the whole situation, consisting of subject and object in their compresence; it is the totality that is true, or good, or beautiful. The value is not subjective, peculiar to the subject like consciousness; nor is it objective, like a secondary quality. It is a subject-object determination.[3]

I do not wish to consider at this juncture the merit of this analysis when restricted to the sphere of human value. I only want to submit a gloss. From one point of view, the analysis reminds one of the attempt to reduce all propositions to the form of subject-predicate relation. The criticism of some contemporary logicians,

1. II, 302.   2. *Ibid.*   3. *Ibid.*, II, 238.

that in many instances the position of the terms in a proposition may be interchanged, is applicable in this connection. Now of course Alexander does not intend the terms subject and object to be taken in any absolute sense. The title to the term is not by prescription. Thus, e.g., to Jill (the subject) Jack (the object) has value or unvalue, depending on whether or not she likes to go tumbling after him; but we must be aware of the fact that Jack also functions as a subject when he functions in relation to Jill (his object). Therefore, when the two things that stand in relation to one another are human, or subhuman, animals, the situation is bidirectional, and it may be that when we consider one thing as the subject, we have one value; and when we consider the other thing (i.e., the erstwhile object) as the subject, we have the unvalue or another value.

There is, however, a sense in which, in Alexander's doctrine, the subject of appreciation is an absolute one, and that is when the social mind is given that status. In that case, the relation between subject and object is one that Russell names asymmetrical.

As for the value-situation on the material or chemical level, it seems fantastic to speak of it as involving a relation between subject and object, and it elucidates nothing. We found that there is significance in pointing to the affinity that subsists among values on all levels; but it should be borne in mind that analogies are not duplications, and therefore, to press an analogy beyond reasonable or poetical bounds, is to confuse rather than clarify.

II. VALUES ON THE PRE-JUDGMENTAL LEVEL

The values of truth, goodness, and beauty emerge with judgment or reflection. We cannot say that they emerge with mind or consciousness, because this empirical quality man shares with other animals, but they do not share with him appreciation of the tertiary qualities.[4] In this section we shall treat of certain instinctive values in man.

Man pursues objects which promote the type, or are necessary to his existence, and these objects are said to have instinctive value. Thus, just as the lion values instinctively its prey, so the child

4. *Ibid.*, II, 304.

values the breast instinctively. We do not commonly regard these objects, in their bareness, as values, and that may be because they are overlaid by the tertiary qualities. But we are not unfamiliar with them; we instinctively approve habits of personal cleanliness, or the coyness of the female. We feel admiration for qualities that further the interests of the type; e.g., courage or pluck, good looks, strength, a hearty appetite. We do not approve of these and their like on moral grounds; but our approbation, Alexander says, is next door to morals. He calls it "instinctive approbation." [5]

We have said that instinctive values are sometimes overlaid by the tertiary qualities or the social values. When this happens to them, they may become the subject-matter of reflective judgment; e.g., when modesty is injured, we judge that modesty is a habit that is a *duty* to oneself. In the case of such social insects as bees, we witness "justice" meted out amongst them, following upon instinctive approbation or disapprobation.

Alexander's treatment of this subject is brief and altogether inadequate. When, for instance, he speaks of the instinctive values being overlaid by the values proper, or the social judgment being grafted upon the instinctive one, he leads one to think that instinctive and reflective values differ in kind, that the latter are not reducible to the former, that they are not emergents therefrom. But such an interpretation runs counter to the entire spirit of his enquiry; yet what link there is between the two classes of value, he does not indicate. The importance of the question is patent; an answer to it may supply a method of investigation into the nature, origin and development of morals, literary types, and other cultural manifestations which constitute the sphere of human values. The use of the method is for the ethnologist, and other specialists, but a consideration of the possibility of the reduction of reflective to instinctive values is a philosophical one.

III. ECONOMIC VALUES

Midway between instinctive and moral values stand the economic values. Instinctive values, we have seen, may blend with moral values; economic values, Alexander seems to think, are and

5. *Ibid.*, II, 305.

remain instinctive, only they exhibit the operation of reflective judgment; although, he adds, they are affected in many ways by moral considerations. Where the only value is living itself, as, e.g., in the Platonic "state of pigs," things have merely instinctive value. But man has not only animal heat; he is a creature that judges, and lives in communities; he therefore has the problem of distribution of goods. This is settled, thinks Alexander, by "the reflective process of demand and supply." [6] Reflection in this process is not used, as in moral valuation, to determine what the moral type shall be, but to secure the most effective distribution within a moral type of social existence already fixed. Morality, then, determines what the type of society shall be. Economics assumes this type and is concerned with the means of sustaining it. The moral values may be described as intrinsic in relation to the economic values, which, in this relation, must be described as instrumental. Thus, e.g., it is a moral problem how far it is right for me to gratify a taste for possessing pictures. Economics determine how much of other commodities I must exchange in order to possess them. But economics always are affected by morals, for morals are effective to change the social type of distribution and to correct the economic inequalities of the existent social type.[7]

This treatment of economic value in *Space, Time, and Deity* is weak and bare. Let us consider several difficulties that it readily suggests. One does not need to turn to the great body of Marxist literature to discover that, if not always, certainly frequently, it is economics that is fundamental to morals rather than that morals are basal to economic values. To agree with Alexander is the equivalent of saying that facts are always dependent on theory. They sometimes are, but more frequently facts are the parents of theory. We cannot go into a full consideration of this important problem, but we want to indicate in brief along what lines Alexander may be refuted.

To take only a single instance, a host of writers have established the fact that in England of the sixteenth and seventeenth centuries the Puritan code of morals was based on an acceptance of the established order of social classes and made its anodyne, its

6. *Ibid.*, II, 306.   7. II, 306–307.

apologist. Tawney has characterized the prevalent religious thought of those centuries as a morality tempered by prudence and occasionally softened by a sentimental compassion for inferiors.[8] Puritanism was a systematic body of religious and moral thought which recognized and approved of the economic virtues. Instead of morality determining what the type of society shall be, and economics assuming the type and supplying the machinery for sustaining it, morals were the handmaid of economics. The only function of the moral and religious teachers seems to have been to act as a *social soporific*. If John Doe was successful in accumulating riches, he was regarded as blessed of God; if Richard Roe was an unsuccessful merchant, or an impoverished laborer, he was told that riches are unimportant for eternal happiness. We know that it is fairly easy to redefine almost any given set of virtues in terms of the qualities which economic success demands. Before the historical period considered above, it was found fairly easy to translate the warrior's ferocity into chivalry, the feudal lord's property into service, the peasant's sweatlabor into vocation. Have we not, in our own economic era, been inclined to call greed enterprise and avarice economy?

It could be shown that morals have their origin in social relations; that social relations are determined by environment, predominantly by technic, or the nature and distribution of the means of production. The social relations make demands on the individuals who participate in them; the demands, because they issue out of relations which are persistent, often repeat themselves and give rise to habits, and ultimately take on the appearance of moral commands, meeting fundamental ever-recurring social needs. Duties are thus basically not conventional but grounded in human needs. They become part of the social surroundings and are transmitted.

Principles of morality become conventional when they break away from their foundations. Thereafter, instead of coöperating with social needs, they become reactionary; they become self-

8. *Religion and the Rise of Capitalism*, 191. We do not mean to suggest that Tawney's view will withstand criticism, but only that it points to a possible approach.

inclosed, systematic; and are governed by the law of contradiction. Then we witness the contradiction between moral theory and practice, the avowal of a morality in public and the practice of its contrary in private. Thus, e.g., might be explained the peculiar regard in which we hold the late President Coolidge; he had the economic virtues of a villager, such as simplicity in his mode of living, frugality, and the like; and he was honored by those who found his precepts inadequate for guidance in our highly technical stage of civilization.

From the foregoing brief analysis it is clear that moral ideals may be of at least two sorts: the ideal which is attained by a backward glance, the morals of our fathers, which we respect but cannot follow; and the ideal which is called forth by opposition to the existing state of affairs in the wills of those whose interests are antagonistic to those of the owning class. The former kind leads to cynicism or hypocrisy; the latter, to dissatisfaction, opposition, the endeavor to bring into being a new social order which shall harmonize with the given material or technical conditions of the natural milieu.

Thus, as against Alexander's view, it might be maintained that the economic condition is the basis, and gives rise to, political and legal forms, and morals; though it is not to be forgotten, as we have pointed out (and with this Alexander agrees), that the forms of the superstructure in their turn react on and influence the development of the economic structure.

As for "the reflective process of demand and supply" securing a distribution of goods so as to maximize the satisfaction of vital wants, probably since, at least, the sixth and seventh centuries B. C., when Thales is said to have cornered the market of olive-presses in Miletus, and sky-rocketed the rental price, this pleasant theory has been held to be not above suspicion.

A curious difficulty is seen in Alexander's statement of the relation that obtains between economic and moral values. When we pass beyond the state of pigs to a society with moral values, our author says, we find that life has ceased to be the only interest; "other interests compete with mere sustenance of life, *though that remains fundamental.*" [9] A few sentences beyond, however, he maintains that morality determines the type of social organization, while economics assume the type and implement machinery for sustaining it. It would appear that if the interest to sustain life is fundamental, then, by derivation, the machinery it will devise in the form of technic and, more particularly, class organization, will also be fundamental.

IV. THE ONTOLOGICAL STATUS OF VALUE

The values proper are creations of mind, or more strictly, belong to the union of the object with the mind. They are mind-dependent. But this dependence in no sense deprives them of reality. True, they are not, in the proper sense, qualities; they are, rather, a new character of reality, which issues from the combination of mind with its object. What Bosanquet thinks to be experience of every kind; namely, something in which mind and its object are distinguishable but inseparable, is true only of the experience of value. Color, e.g., is independent of mind and exists in total separation from it; but the color's beauty is the resultant of the indissoluble amalgamation of mind with the color. Its beauty is a character superadded to it from its relation to mind.

It therefore follows that though the values proper, i.e., truth, goodness, and beauty, are spoken of by Alexander as tertiary qualities, they are not properly qualities.

It might be contended that if values depend on mind, are mental creations, they are, therefore, unreal. Their analogy with illusory appearances occurs. Illusory appearances occupy a status between veridical images and errors, and are in themselves, as mere appearances, perspectives of the real world from the point of view of a diseased mind. Alexander says "they are objective and nonmental and owe to the mind nothing but their selection from the real world." [10] They have all the characters of reality, and become errors only when believed in; e.g., as when I say that the gray paper that looks green is really green. In Alexander's view, then, illusions are not unreal. They become unreal when believed. Until belief is injected, it is simply a dislocation of elements which

9. II, 307. Italics supplied.   10. II, 236.

are themselves real, "a mentally distorted perspective of the real." [11]

But there are unrealities, and they are of several kinds. There are empirical unrealities, like the golden mountain, "which is as a matter of fact unreal"; [12] categorial unrealities, like the round square, which, though it can be entertained in thought, is self-contradictory and impossible; and there is a class of unrealities which is intermediate, like a mare's nest.

Where, in a Space-Time universe, do these unrealities have their being? Does the real world contain errors and illusions *as such?* The conception is self-contradictory; for by error we mean something rejected by the world of reality.

Alexander's position is that there is no class of objects which belong only to the mental world; though, of course, he believes that primary and secondary qualities belong only to the physical world. But there is a class of objects which belong to both the mental and physical worlds, in the sense that they would not exist if there were no psychical or no material realm. In this class—which has its analogue in Russell's "neutral stuff" [13]—belong illusions, values, and the unvalues—error, badness, ugliness.

We would expect that if illusory appearances do not forfeit their title to reality, certainly values should not; and Alexander, as we have said, does claim the character of reality for the values. It would be very strange, indeed, he argues, if the issue of the marriage of two realities should itself be an unreality. Values result from the amalgamation of mind and its objects. Mind, in Alexander's system, is the highest finite reality we know. "Strange," he remarks, "that its touch should be thought to derealise its creations." [14] To think the contrary, he maintains, is to show oneself laboring under a misconception which is the lingering on of an old tradition. When the ideas of primary qualities were believed to be copies of reality, and the ideas of the secondary qualities merely the effects in our minds produced by the realities, only the primary qualities were real, and the secondary ones were subjective and said to be unreal. Thus it might be thought, also, that values, since

11. II, 225. 12. II, 224.
13. *The Analysis of Mind*, Lecture I. 14. II, 245.

they admittedly do not exist without minds, are similarly subjective, having nothing in reality corresponding to them. But for
Alexander mind is one of the realities, itself a complex of Space-
Time stuff. Values, therefore, "arise in the relation of these realities to other realities, in virtue of which a fresh reality is constituted." [15]

As an example of a reality which is compounded of mind and a
non-mental thing, yet not a value, is the "person," which is neither
the subject-self alone nor the object-self alone, but the union of
the two, that is, the body taken together with the consciousness
of it or the consciousness along with the body which is its object.
Similarly, the realities which are the objects of the appreciation of
value are organic to mind, and value, strictly, belongs to the compound whole.

Values thus have a mental character, which, once for all, dif-
ferentiates them from the qualities. While qualities are selected
by mind, the selection is from the thing itself. But values, though
founded in reality, are themselves the results of our selection. The
value of a thing is not in the thing itself, but is born in the act of
appreciation. They are human inventions; but their materials are
independent of the inventor. [16] The value is in the object only in
so far as the valuing subject possesses or appreciates it. It belongs
to the object as it is possessed by the mind and not outside that
relation. The appreciation by mind is, therefore, a *sine qua non*
needed to make the object with which it stands in relation true or
good or beautiful.

In our exposition thus far we have stressed the importance, for
the genesis and maintenance of value, of the mental side of the
relation. But values have an objective character. Their basis is not
only mind's imputation. Although it does not exist apart from the
subject, value is a property of the object distinguishable from the
act of appreciation. Mind is needed to give the object the character of truth, goodness, or beauty, or their opposites, but in the
object itself there is a corresponding character, of which we become aware in our appreciations. Let us consider the value beauty
in an object. It is not merely the ability of a thing to please us

15. *Ibid.*   16. II, 243.

generally, in virtue of its sensible or other qualities. Beauty is a character in the thing which pleases us in a certain way, i.e., in such a way as to call for the appreciative aesthetic judgment. It follows, that this character is possessed by the object over and above the characters which it has as an object of sense or thought; and it is this character that is the object of the act of appreciation.

The singularity of the aesthetic character in the object appears when contrasted with the feeling of pleasantness it induces. We say that sugar is pleasant because it gives pleasure; "to call it pleasant means nothing more than this." [17] We do not suppose that, in addition to its taste, there is in the sugar a quality of pleasantness. If we were not to taste the sugar, there would be no pleasantness in it. But beauty, as we have said, is not simply the ability to please us. While the appreciation of the beauty of a thing is a pleasing act of mind, it is not at all identical with the pleasantness. And while the qualities in the sugar which made it pleasant are actually in the sugar *irrespective of the mind to which it gives bodily pleasure*,[18] aesthetic appreciation is a reaction to something in the object itself, *only it is not in the object until mind appreciates it.*[19]

V. THE REALITY OF VALUES

If this exposition is not free from obscurities, we may pass on the blame to our source. Our author's views on this head lack clarity, and his expressions are frequently paradoxical, and sometimes, perhaps, even contradictory.

Consider, e.g., his view that values are real, i.e., part and parcel of the universe of Space-Time. This suggests, as we have indicated, a comparison with his view that illusory appearances are also real, in the sense defined, because they are made up of elements which belong to the real world, and only the selection of them and their combination is the mind's work.

Now, to maintain, on the grounds stated, that illusions are part of the real world of Space-Time, is, we submit, to work the realistic doctrine to the death. If what is real is Space-Time and whatever occupies it, and appearances are said to be illusory when

17. II, 242.   18. II, 243.   19. II, 242.

they do not *truly* occupy Space-Time,[20] the conclusion inevitably follows that they are *therefore* unreal.

To say that illusions are unreal is not to imply that they belong to a world outside the real world of Space-Time. We know no other world. What we mean is that they are rejected by the real world. Rejection does not necessarily mean transference. In the case of illusions it means only that mind must retain them, since the external world will not have them. To argue that illusions are objective and non-mental because made up of elements which in separation are each of them objective and non-mental, is to miss the point *why they are called illusions*. It is not the *elements* in their apartness which present the problem for the perceiver, but their *combination*. So far as he is concerned, and as far as Space-Time as the world of realty is concerned, the situation would not be the more complicated were the elements, too, in separation, purely subjective and mental. The illusion, *as such*, would not be *more* of an illusion.

Our concern with the nature of illusory appearances is not tangential, for Alexander is right, that, if you admit *them* as real, we may have no difficulty concerning values; for both values and illusions are of a class of objects which belong to both the mental and physical worlds, arise only if mind and matter are wedded.

Alexander avoids characterizing values and illusions as unreal, not because he does not admit the legitimacy of the concept, for, as we have seen, he admits that error is unreal; but, rather, for the unexpressed reason, that a metaphysic, whose premises lead to the conclusion that that which man holds dearest and most significant is unreal, condemns itself as spun out of gossamer and spiderweb. The reason that he assigns; namely, that mind is the highest finite reality we know, and it is, therefore, unthinkable that its touch should derealise its creations,[21] is not a powerful one, for he admits as we have said, that errors are unreal; and are *they* anything but the derealised creations of that selfsame highest finite reality?

The comparison of value with illusion, however, while instructive, must not be pressed far. If illusions are real, it might be con-

20. II, 236.   21. II, 245.

cluded that values are *a fortiori* real; yet the converse may not be true; viz., values may be real and illusory appearances unreal.

It should, however, be said here, by way of a caveat, that we do not suppose the word "real" to have any magic in it. Eddington somewhere remarks that the term is frequently used as though it were some kind of celestial halo, with the intention that it evoke in us some sentiment. Thus we sometimes are led to speak of a *real* experience; as if *any* experience could be *un*real. In philosophy such usage is unwarranted. We do not want to honor or degrade values; only to discover what is their nature. Nor need it be feared that the conclusion that values are unreal will be effective to dispel them, anymore than the finding that illusions are unreal is guarantee against their recurrence or increase.

It is our thought that in Alexander may be found two definitions of reality, a circumstance which inevitably leads to confusion and much questioning. "The real," he says, "is Space-Time as a whole and every complex or part within it." [22] From this all-inclusive, so to speak omnivorous definition, it would follow that unreality is a concept with possibly only a regulative function. Everything is real, for there is *no thing* extrinsic to, or outside the pale of, Space-Time. Therefore, illusions and values are no less real than the categories and qualities. But the real is also used in a more restricted sense; viz., to characterize objects "in so far as they are apprehended as parts of Space-Time distinct from ourselves." [23] The real, in this sense, is the non-mental. Thus, in discussing illusory appearances in a section other than the one from which we previously quoted, we find Alexander judges them by reference to the latter test. "Some of our objects are illusory," he says; "they are real as far as they are perspectives of Space-Time, but they contain an element introduced by our personality, and do not belong where they seem to belong." [24] He does not *say* these appearances are unreal; but does he need to?

Regarding values, they are real in Alexander's system in so far as they are part of the universe of Space-Time. In so far, however, as values depend on mind for their origin and being, belong strictly to an amalgamation or union of subject and object, they are not,

22. II, 247.   23. *Ibid.*   24. II, 249.

in the limited sense of the term, real. Yet we find our author maintaining without qualification that the tertiary qualities, "though they differ from the secondary and primary ones in being creations of mind, are not the less real." [25]

We believe that in recording the ambiguity we have pursued the question far enough and probably exhausted its importance. Values are real in one sense and unreal in another, and the problem is strictly one of definition. We recall the dispute between Alice and Humpty Dumpty. "When *I* use a word," he said scornfully, "it means just what I choose to mean—neither more nor less." "The question is," she answered, "whether you *can* make words mean so many different things." "The question is," replied Humpty Dumpty, "which is to be master—that's all."

VI. WHERE IS VALUE RESIDENT?

We do need, however, to consider just where value resides. On this point, too, Alexander is not precise. Values are not qualities of reality, in the same sense that color, or form, or mind, or life is a quality.[26] They are a new character of reality, *values,* which arise through the combination of mind with its object. In the value-experience mind and its object can be distinguished but not separated; subject and object are in indissoluble union, and they give birth to a fresh reality. "Strictly speaking," he says, "it is this compound whole to which value belongs." [27] We have seen, however, that he also says that value is in the object itself, only it is not in the object until the mind appreciates it.[28]

There is an absence of nicety here; but the two views are reconcilable if they be taken to refer to different phases of the subject. Alexander does not himself make the distinction, but the interpolation or gloss is necessary if it is thought desirable to save his expressions from the stigma of self-contradiction. It can be maintained, it is our view, that the *genesis* of value is in the compound whole of subject-object relation; but once created, and maintained by the compound, value is in the object.[29]

25. II, 244.   26. II, 237.   27. II, 246.   28. II, 242.
29. In this connection by subject is meant the social mind. Otherwise it could not be said that the value is in any sense in the object; for if its

Analyze any experience whatever and you will find two distinct elements and their relation to one another. The two terms of the relation are, on the one hand, the act of mind, and, on the other, the object of which the mind is aware. The relation is the compresence of mind and object; their togetherness, which connects two distinct existences into the total situation called the experience.[30] How is the togetherness in the knowing relation experienced? Consider, e.g., my seeing a horse. I do not contemplate the horse's togetherness with myself, but, rather, I enjoy my togetherness with the horse. I do not enjoy *the horse as seen,* but *the horse as such.* What I see is not a horse which I see to be together with me; I experience my togetherness with the horse, which I express by saying that I see the horse. This is the experience of togetherness from the point of view of the being which has the experience, that is, the mind.

How is the togetherness experienced by the angel? From his point of view, "I am together with the horse I see and the horse together with me, we are together both." [31] The angel experiences the compresence of two objects, while I experience the compresence of an enjoying mind and the contemplated non-mental object.

This distinction between the angel's experience and the mind's in the knowing relation may be made also in the appreciating or valuing relation. In the knowing relation, Alexander says, "the horse as seen or the seen horse is a description of the horse from the philosopher's point of view in discussing the matter, not from the point of view of the experient himself." [32] It seems to us that to speak of value as residing in the compound itself of subject-related-to-object is to adopt the angelic view to the exclusion of the view of a human mind. It is true—but only as the angel's view. To say that it is the compound whole to which value belongs is on

existence were dependent on the presence of the individual subject in the relation, then the value would be in the object now and absent later, or be and not be in the object simultaneously, as would be the case if Richard Roe appreciates the value and John Doe does not. We wish it to be understood that the discussion is offered as a gloss on Alexander, and is not an attempt to state the critic's position. It suggests a way of saving Alexander's various views from the stigma of inconsistency.

30. I, 11–12.   31. I, 21.   32. *Ibid.*

a par with saying that it is the compound whole to which the knowing relation belongs.

From the mind's viewpoint, just as it knows the horse *as horse* and not as *seen horse*, so it appreciates a value as *the value* and not as the *value appreciated*.

From the angelic viewpoint, then, value is the entire situation of subject-object-relation. The situation has value or is a value-situation by reason of being such a situation. Absent one of the terms, and the value disappears, because the situation has disintegrated.

From the experient's viewpoint, however, value is where he finds it, and that is always in the object. Good is not in me but in my conduct, the object at the performance of which I strain. To you, I may be a good man; but to you I am an object. Beauty is in the music and not in the state which it induces in me; for I can, conceivably, take an opiate which will induce the same emotional state, and yet I will call neither the drug nor the effect beautiful. To tell me that the beauty is in me is really to tell me something I do not know nor ever will. That is your angelic report, not my humble one. Meredith's "Song of the Songless," with the burden that the sedges do not sing except in my heart, may be good metaphysics but is bad aesthetics.

There is, of course, from Alexander's standpoint, a marked difference between the knowing and the valuing situations; and that is, that in the former, what we see is really out there, an object of a definite shape and certain colors, etc., and its *esse* is not dependent on my *percipi;* while in the latter, *esse* is *percipi*, for apart from the mind or valuing subject there is no value.

The distinction is an important one, but we fail to note its significance in the present connection. Consider, e.g., the blush on a girl's cheek when a boy eyes her keenly. Let the boy begone, or fail to look at her, and the blush will not be in her cheek. This is a case in which, preëminently, *to be* means to be *perceived*. The angel will tell you that the blush is the whole situation of boy and girl in relation to one another. But only the angel can give this description. To everyone else, even to the girl herself, the blush was in her cheek. If the dancer is applauded for her aesthetic performance, she, too, like her spectators, knows that the beauty was in her dance; and if roses could talk, like beautiful ladies, they would congratulate themselves on their wondrous grace and loveliness. This is not incompatible with the belief that a rose cannot blush when unseen; that flowers do not "waste their sweetness on the desert air"; that ladies are not beautiful except thinking makes them so.

The argument from the relativity of values to their subjectivity can have little appeal to the realist. To the idealist, at least since Berkeley, primary qualities are as relative, and, therefore, as subjective, as the secondary; *a fortiori* values. But to Alexander, secondary qualities are as objective and non-relative as the primary are to Locke. Regarding values, while he denies that they can exist in a situation in which mind is not a partner, we see no reason why he cannot maintain that *in* the mind-object relation, value is as objective and non-relative as the secondary qualities.

Such a theory, we believe, is in agreement, also, with our practice. If we fail to appreciate Bach's toccatas, we do not condemn them as ugly or indifferent, or disregard their existence entirely; for we recognize the fault to be in us; no less than when, being color-blind, we fail to distinguish between two colors. And if yesterday we appreciated their beauty and fail to do so today, we do not say that they have suffered a change, but that something has gone amiss in us, our sense is not properly attuned, for we do not appreciate properly the beauty that is *in* them.

As for the question whether value can be the relation itself, this is hardly conceivable if relation is bare compresence. Nor is value a character of the relation, for relation is without character; it is not a subject of qualities or characters.

VII. VALUES AS SOCIAL AND JUDGMENTAL

We have seen that appreciation of value arises out of the relation of compresence of mind and object. How do we know this? We have said that, given this relation, value is in the object. But value is not relative to my mind, a subjective character; it is like the primary and secondary qualities in its objectivity. Why do we insist that value is generated only in the subject-object-relation situation, and needs this situation for its maintenance, but make no such analysis in the case of the qualities?

This is because, as we shall see, appreciations arise from the community of minds, out of intercourse between minds. A solitary mind, if such a monstrosity is conceivable, would find itself merely set against objects with which it is compresent. He would make mistakes of sense or judgment, and acting on them in practice, would find that the facts were different, and would change his mind, if he survived his mistake. His mistakes would be misadventures, but he would not say he was in error. He would abandon his belief without thinking about the matter. "He would not be aware of an error, for he would only know that the reality was not as he thought it to be; he would only notice that things were not so, not that it was his mind, his believing, which was at fault." [33] He becomes aware that a proposition is false only when he finds it entertained by another, and his own judgment is in disagreement with it. [34] When his fellow entertains the belief which the reality rejects, he says, It is your mind or your believing that is at fault; your belief not only fails to work, but it is an error. Thus he learns what error is, the product of mind and reality, and thereafter he can consider his own belief as if he himself, in entertaining it, were another person, and judge his belief not only as an ineffective tool but as an error. In the absence of the other mind, he would not notice his own. To suppose that he would be aware of error though his mind were never in intercourse with another, is to commit the mistake of "introjection"; "it is to read into ourselves what we discover in fact from observation of others. We treat ourselves as if without others we could discover in ourselves what we only discover from them." [35] It is, then, only after we have witnessed other minds in error, that we are aware that it is not merely possible for us to make mistakes, "but that an error may be somehow a real existence." [36] Thereafter, turning our minds upon ourselves, we judge ourselves with the eyes of the community; see ourselves as others see us, and recognize our errors as such. We need other minds for thinking truly, so that we may learn the very contrast of true and false thinking.

33. II, 260–1.   34. II, 239.   35. II, 261.   36. II, 239.

That there is no good or bad, in a moral sense, simply for the individual as a solitary creature, is even more obvious. My appreciation, as a moral good, of a certain end or object attained by conduct, arises in social intercourse, in which are presented persons who have willed ends or objects compatible or incompatible with mine. We approve certain objects and secure them, or we secure certain objects which are disapproved. "It is by this contrast between different ends and the wills for them that the appreciation of good and bad arises." [37]

Regarding beauty, in what sense it, too, involves, in Alexander's doctrine, reference to other minds, it is no easy matter to discover. All values, he maintains, depend on propositions, or judgments; and judging and sociality are convertible.[38] Indeed, the sociality is displayed or expressed in language or propositions. The perspectives of reality before the mind take the form of judgments. Judging and sociality are convertible; for, in judgment, the object or proposition judged comes, as we have seen, into relations of agreement or conflict with the judgments of other persons. "Language is the direct communication with one another about our objects. Even our percepts when described become judgments. Judgment accordingly contains in itself a social suggestion, and a judgment of value is intrinsically social." [39]

The connection between the aesthetic value and sociality may be seen, perhaps, more clearly through judgment than directly. "Even the beautiful thing," he says, "though an object of perception, depends on judgments." [40]

We have seen that the true and the good are not simply some things which satisfy, but things which satisfy in a way which can be shared by other minds. Indeed, the sharing was presupposed to the satisfaction. Now this is also true of beauty, for the perception of beauty is the result of judgment; and judgment, to repeat, is founded in sociality. Alexander does not mean that in apprehending beauty, we first make the judgment, This is beautiful. He means something altogether different. Let us explain.

Suppose we are looking at, say, the picture of an animal. We perceive the external object, and if we judge or feel it to be beauti-

37. II, 240.   38. II, 295-6, 303-4.   39. II, 304.   40. II, 303-4.

ful, that is only possible if the imagination has detached itself from the percept and has seen the painted form as alive. The feeling of beauty implies the judgment, I see this painted form alive. It is because this judgment is implied in the beautiful work, that it is possible for other minds to notice my attitude and to find the same object beautiful and share my attitude.[41]

At this juncture it is necessary to refer to another usage by Alexander of the term sociality, which is to be sharply differentiated from the meaning already defined. It is only to him who reads Alexander with great care that the equivocation is apparent, for the author himself seems unaware of it.

We have said that we become aware of the falsity of a proposition when we find it entertained by another and our own judgment disagrees with his; the very possibility of appreciation arises from the community of minds. In a passage which we have already cited,[42] Alexander says that after our discovery of error in another's mind,

> when, with this consciousness, this acquaintance with error, we turn our minds upon ourselves, we can judge ourselves with the eyes of the community, and recognize that we are or were in error. We judge ourselves, in enjoyment, as if we were in our mistake another person. In our better mind about the same reality we represent the collective mind, and our worse mind was then the victim of error for us, and the object of its belief an error or erroneous. Thus we do not merely need other minds to supply us with facts which may escape our notice because of our short life and limited opportunities. We need them for thinking truly in order that we may learn the very contrast of thinking truly and falsely.

It seems that he intends to say that only in the conflict of minds is truth *revealed;* that it is only by virtue of my private mind being a member of a community of minds that I learn to distinguish truth from error or falsity; that the participation of my mind in a group of minds is the *occasion* for the differentiation of truth and error; that truth and error are for the private mind, but the recog-

41. II, 294-5. 42. II, 239.

nition of them is dependent on my mind's having intercourse with other minds. But he says more: that true knowledge owes its truth to the collective mind; that it is the collective mind which determines what in my private mind is true and what false; that it is the standard or test, not simply the occasion.

The failure to distinguish sharply these two uses of the concept of sociality leads Alexander to considerable confusion in his treatment of each of the qualities.

CHAPTER 4

Meaning and Value

OUR EXPOSITION brings us to a special consideration of each of the tertiary qualities. Before we treat of them, however, it is advisable to inquire into the nature of meaning, having in view primarily the problem of the relation of meaning and the aesthetic value.

Alexander does not have a complete theory of meaning and nowhere deals with the subject specially. In this section we shall attempt to give an exposition of his views as they appear in the chapters on "The Clue to Quality" and on "Mind and Knowing," in the second volume of *Space, Time, and Deity.*

All mental action implies the relation of a subject to an object. Meaning is the reference to the object, "and in this sense every conscious process means or refers to an object other than the mental process itself." [1] Meaning is a conscious condition of mind; it is in mind, and *refers* to something not in mind. It is the act of reference to something not in the mind itself. There is no act of mind without such reference; every act of mind contains a reference to something distinct from the mind.[2]

There are two senses of meaning to be distinguished. There is, *first,* the meaning in extension; as when I point to a person and say, I mean you. It is reference to an object; and it is in this sense of the term that what we have said is true; namely, that every conscious process means or refers to an object other than the mental process itself.

Now the object need not necessarily be one perceived and pres-

1. II, 15.   2. II, 97.

ent to the senses; it may be an ideal one, like a purpose to go to London, or even an imaginary object.

The meaning of a word in extension is the reference to the actual thing to which it is applied. The meaning is the intellectual substitute for pointing to it. It tells of a thing or condition or source different from the presentation, but revealed by it.

There is, *secondly*, the meaning in intension. In this sense, the meaning of a word is the reference to the ideas it conveys; the characters of the things it names. A part of a complex whole means the rest of the complex; thus, the sight of a marble means its coldness, the knight on the chess-board means the moves which I may make with it, the first words of a line mean for me the rest.

It is obvious that under intensional meaning Alexander groups two distinct mental acts that ought to be differentiated. Why he thinks them both intensional, does not appear. In *one* sense, it refers to the conceptual, the pervasive characteristic, the identical quality,—the connotative meaning. In this sense, a word refers to the universal it stands for. To Alexander concepts are in the same class with presentations and are real appearances of the source which conditions them; for they are configurations of Space-Time, in *pari materia* with sensa, images, or percepta,[3] and are external, non-mental.[4]

Thus, a word refers to an individual object which it names (the extensional or denotative meaning) or to the universal, pervasive character which a number of objects have in common (the intensional or connotative meaning).

The *second* sense in which a thing may be said to have intensional meaning is that which, I think, should preferably be called its systematic meaning. The sight of the marble means its coldness, the first words of a line mean for me the rest. Things are only partially presented in sense; they are part sensed and part ideated. Thus I have seen, felt, and smelt an orange at one and the same time. Now I only see it; its feel and fragrance are ideal. What were before sensa have become ideata; similarly, what was before an ideatum, may now be a sensum. In the relation of mind and the things of the external world, objects are only partial revelations

3. II, 96.   4. I, 24; II, 76, 250.

of things. In vision, strictly, I apprehend only a patch of yellow color of a certain configuration, but because experience is synthetic, I say that I see an orange, supplying in ideation the various other features of it which I have cognized previously.[5]

What we perceive is things and not sensations, and things are always systems. Sensations are always subordinated to the thing and are often altogether indistinguishable. Things, as we have intimated, are the results of much organized experience. Rather than the effect of the stimulus, things are the organized reactions thereto. Professor Pillsbury has said that the nearest approach to bare sensation is found in the after-image, contrast colors, and other processes of the sort that have no meaning in the outside world. And even these imply some reference to earlier organized experience before they may be appreciated; and so they cannot be called absolutely raw material. Perception is always of a thing, and the thing is not for psychology a mass of sensations or a mass of movements, but a type, or a concept, or, as we prefer to call it, a system.[6]

Now, while it is useful to distinguish these three senses in which things, words, are said to mean; namely, the extensional, intensional, and systematic,—it is to be noted that the first two participate in the last. If universals are as real as individuals, as objective and independent, a word can point to a universal no less than to a particular thing. The difference lies not in the nature of the mental function but of the referents. We shall return to this subject later, and attempt to show that the extensional is only a species of systematic meaning. That Alexander should have distinguished the (strictly) intensional from the systematic meaning, appears when he attempts to show that intensional meaning (in his broad sense) is to be explained in terms of neural processes—and the examples he gives all involve only systematic meaning. Let us turn to his treatment of the correspondence of meaning to neural processes.

He rejects the possibility of explaining meaning by "mere indifferent lines of association."[7] Mental life, he maintains, is mental

5. I, 13–15, 23, 25, 40–1, 115–130, 127; II, 86, 90, 183, 212.
6. *Vide,* Pillsbury, "The Role of the Type in Simple Mental Processes," 20 *Phil. Rev.* 498, at 506–7.   7. II, 16.

processes arranged in various complicated patterns, and a word
sets going in my brain and in my mind that pattern of process
which we call the meaning. Thought may be imageless, "customs
of mind which may also be customs in the neural structure, not
mere neural statical dispositions, but those neural exercises of a
habit which are identical with the consciousness of a thought
without its necessary embodiment in sense." [8] As examples of his
thought he cites the following: When the exercise of the habit is
become specific and detailed, we may have the meaning turn into
an illustration or concrete embodiment of the meaning, as when
the word horse not only makes me think of horse, "but of the
particular foal whose affection I attach to myself in the country by
the offer of sugar"; or, when the marble looks cold, "the very
essence of the condition of my mind is that the sight process is
qualified by the ideal touch process, and the transition from one
to the other is in my mind"; or, when I see an orange and think of
Sicily, that is because the two are woven into a complex; or, finally,
when I use a word like "government," there is set going in my
brain and mind a whole complicated neuro-physical pattern, transitive and elusive, because wanting in detail, and though I may go
on and fill out the transitive outline, with the pictures of the coali-
tion ministry, "it is still the elusive complex which stands out as
the main occupation of my mind." [9]

In each of the examples it will be seen that what is illustrated is
that a part of a complex whole means the rest of the complex—the
part having systematic meaning.

Several criticisms may be made of our author's treatment of
the topic under consideration. *First*, that, instead of systematic
meaning being a species of intensional meaning, it is the genus of
which extensional meaning is a species; *secondly*, that neural
processes are no less indifferent than "mere indifferent lines of
association." We shall treat of these criticisms seriatim.

A. A thing, word, perception, sensum, etc., has sytematic meaning when by reference it is taken to mean the rest of the complex
of which it is a part. Now, in what sense other than this has it an
extensional meaning? If cow means to me my black-eyed varie-

8. II, 17.   9. *Ibid.*

gated Susan, it is only because the two, the cow and the idea are fragments of a whole of which they individually are parts. While images can be supplanted by conventional signs in the mind, when the conventional sign means by extension, it does so only by translating itself into an image; and the image and the thing meant are no less fragments of one experience, than my sight of the orange's color and my idea of its taste. If words do point to things, it is only because they participate in a world in which words and things comprise a congenial company. The child sees a round lighted object in the heavens, and hears its mother say it is the moon as she points to it. Thereafter the object and the sound are linked, and when the earth's satellite appears in its field of vision it will cry, Moon, Moon; just as, seeing an orange, it will cry for its juice. Extensional meaning, then, is systematic meaning when that which is said to have meaning is a sound which has been conventionalized into a word.

The validity of this analysis becomes patent when we consider an onomatopoeic word. We hear a bark and we think of a dog. We see the word "Woof" in a book for children, and we tell little Nell that the dog in the book is asking for his bone. The two instances are on a par; then why should the word lose its systematic nature and assume another by admittance into the columns of the dictionary? True, few of the dictionary words are, in their present advanced stage certainly, onomatopoeic; *but they function as if they were: for their meaning is only what they evoke.* Systematic meaning, then, instead of being a species of intensional meaning, is the class of which extensional meaning is an instance.

B. Alexander rejects association because it works on "mere indifferent lines." Now, his explanation of meaning in terms of correspondence with neural processes may be a desirable feature when considered from the psychological or metaphysical viewpoint; but it needs to be emphasized that the substitution *does not eliminate the element of indifference.* Whatever principle is selected, the fact still remains that there is no way of preventing anything from serving as a symbol for almost any other thing. The lines, before they become marked, are indifferent, whether they be neural or otherwise.

A thing has meaning when it causes one to think of something else. By a thing, in this context, is meant not only objects in Space-Time, such as a red light or railroad gates, but also ideas; and ideas include images, concepts, percepts, etc.

But a thing may make one think of any number of things which another mind would judge irrelevant and misleading. One is frequently led to think of the wrong things; even of evil things while one is listening to a pious sermon. Mention of the word "sound" to a young poet who finds himself in a physics laboratory may cause him to think of a bird's call or the wind rustling autumn leaves; or, meeting Peter, I may think of Paul who resembles him, and say, thinking of Paul, "Do you recall, Peter, when you and I went fishing together?"

Perhaps it would be better if, in accordance with the ideal of the mathematical logicians, symbol-meaning-thing were united in indissoluble union; but, as we shall see, this may very well be doubted. At any rate, we must accept it as a fact that meanings are not fixed; for the meaning in one context is supplanted by another meaning in another context.

It may be said that a person knows *the* meaning of a thing when he uses it in circumstances which would lead others to use it and in a similar manner. We look upon a mind as deranged when it habitually gives to things meanings they do not have to others. But, fortunately, the line between absolute sanity and absolute insanity is of infinite divisibility.

It cannot be denied that things do have a conventional meaning. A chair means something to sit on; a red light as a traffic signal means Stop; American means a native of America. But we characterize a person who thinks only of the conventional meanings as a prosy soul, an innocent, one who in the eighteenth century would be described as "simple, but honest." I dare say we are much more interested in, e.g., Mr. G. B. Shaw, to whom American means a nincompoop, a booby; that is to say, in meanings which no one but an *un*conventional mind would think,—meanings which are found not in dictionaries, but in diaries.[10]

10. In science meaning is thought to be in some sense intrinsic to the symbol. The cause means necessarily, not arbitrarily, the effect. Mind is not

The point is this: that the fact remains the same whatever principle or explanation is chosen. It may be possible to explain meaning as the mental correspondent of neural processes; yet the meaning relation between symbol and thing will still be along lines merely indifferent. It is no disproof of associationism that symbols in meaning situations are shamelessly promiscuous, now mating themselves with one thing and now with another, as fancy likes.

Certain results follow from our analysis and criticism of the theory of meaning. *First*, that the meaning situation implies the activity of mind. Apart from mind there is no meaning. Meanings are in symbols and for mind. *Secondly*, that things and ideas, in so far as they have meaning, are symbolic, stand for something other than themselves. Meaning is through symbol to the thing meant. Meaning is therefore a transaction in mind between symbol and object. *Third*, because any idea or thing may come to mean any object, meaning is always from a point of view or aspect of mind. This is also true because a thing is always more than what it means to me. *Fourth*, that meaning is systematic or intensional.

When we come to treat of beauty, it will be seen that Alexander's view is that the aesthetic situation is in the main free of meaning. It is advisable, therefore, at this point, to inquire if there is a sphere of mental activity to which meaning is stranger. Alexander supplies no theoretical discussion of this question; it is, therefore, necessary for us to do this, offering a theory which we think is consistent with his views on aesthetics and a theoretical foundation therefor.

Knowledge is always representative, because it makes use of meaning. Knowledge is never direct. Unless, however, one is a Platonist, it is clear that knowledge must be founded ultimately on a direct experience. This experience is perception. Perception to Alexander is always direct.[11] We see precisely what a thing is; not through a Lockeian idea or any other instrument or veil, but immediately. Immediate awareness is not, properly, knowledge, be-

---

willful, and gives no orders. It functions only to discover; and it learns by following. Of this we shall treat at greater length (than is here possible) in the chapter on Truth.

11. II, Book III, ch. VI, especially p. 157.

cause it is not symbolic,—the object of direct perception has no meaning and is not meant; it is just itself. You must take it or leave it; you can ask no questions of it or concerning it. Knowledge, therefore, presupposes logically prior and independent awareness of things themselves. In knowledge we know *through* symbols; in awareness, we are aware *of* the thing before us. (Of course, we must be *aware* of the things through which we *know*.) Knowledge, then, is symbolic, and indirect; awareness is immediate and non-symbolic—it is an actual seizure of the object by the mind in experience. Meanings are ultimately grounded in experiences which do not mean. As we have said, this distinction between immediate awareness and knowledge through meaning is accepted *sub silentio* by Alexander, and plays an important part in his aesthetic theory.

We wish to call attention here to several difficulties this position presents. We have already said that Alexander's view is that experience is always synthetic. One day I only see the orange, the next day I touch it, and finally I also taste it. Each special feature has been cognized separately; but now when I see the object, the other features are also suggested to me. But from this we are not to infer that an object can be ever given in segregation.

> The partial revelation of a thing to mind in the form of objects which belong to the thing merely means in the end that no object, nor even a thing, is given alone, but, because it is a part of Space-Time, coheres in varying degrees of closeness with other objects and groups of such objects connected together by the categorial relation of substance, that is, belonging to the same volume of space-time. One object may suggest the others which participate with it in the one substance: that is, it means the others and may be said, though only loosely, to refer to them. Moreover, no object is apprehended except as being the whole or a part of the space-time which contains them all. Thus even the patch of yellow is seen extended over the space which is part of the orange. No object therefore is apprehended by itself but points to other finites as well. It is spread over the space which is apprehended with it.[12]

12. II, 94.

It is clear, then, that experience is always synthetic. From this it follows that no mental act is ever experienced in which there is no systematic meaning. But there is a further difficulty.

It is of the nature of the categories that they are pervasive characters which belong in some form to all existents whatever. *Even mind possesses these characters.*[13] Among the categories are the universal, the particular and the individual. We would expect, then, to find that there is no experience in which the category of universality fails to participate; and if we are not disappointed, it would follow that there is no mental act from which there is absent intensional meaning, or reference to a universal feature.

In a significant passage Alexander recognizes this implication, and admits that even in sensation there is a universal element.

> In any sensory process (or in any other mental process) there are the categorial feature of existence as a particular and the categorial feature of subsistence, or existence as a universal. The same distinction is found in the object or sensum. . . . From the beginning of psychical life the universal and particular are united. . . . In other words, though sensing is not thinking, there is no sensation without its universal or thought.[14]

He adds in a footnote [15] that the above appears to say the same thing as Aristotle's dictum that we perceive the particular, but perception is of such-and-such.

It appears, then, that in every mental act there is meaning in both its senses; namely, systematic and intensional. This is the view that finds expression in *Space, Time, and Deity*. As we have said, Alexander's treatment of the aesthetic experience (in subsequent publications) points to a radical departure from this position. He does not attempt to reconcile the two views, and we hazard the opinion that the thing cannot be done. On the one hand we have the view that the aesthetic experience is one of pure awareness, in which meaning plays no part at all, in which there is an identification of medium and content—an identification because it is not possible to distinguish them within that experience. On the other hand, there is the view that in every mental process there is the synthesis of part

13. I, 185.　　　　14. II, 131, 132.　　　　15. P. 132.

with part, and the union of two categorial features, i.e., of the universal and the particular; thus both systematic and intensional meaning.

It is undoubted that, having in mind his system generally, the latter position, that is, the one maintained in *Space, Time, and Deity*, is the only one maintainable. The metaphysical difficulties that the former one suggests could find no solution in his philosophy. For one thing, the implication is that universals and particulars have nothing in common, that the two realms are disjointed. Another difficulty would be to bridge the gap between awareness and knowledge; meaning would be not only unique but miraculous. Thirdly, if there is no such thing as a *pure* sensation, how can there be pure awareness?

We do not, however, mean to imply, that his views that appear in *Space, Time, and Deity* are themselves consistent one with the other. The position, e.g., that perception is direct seems an impossible one if all knowledge is concededly systematic, hence mediated or representative. Maybe a raw material (whatever that may be) of experience might be said to be apprehended directly; but even so, it is not *known* in the character in which it is apprehended (howsoever that experience may be described). There seems to be no middle ground between epistemological monism and epistemological dualism. To certify to both, as Alexander seems to do, without the attempt being made to reconcile them, seems to be a piece of unwarranted dogmatism. But this is not the occasion on which to pursue this subject further.

CHAPTER 5

Beauty

I. BEAUTY AS A SUBJECT-OBJECT RELATION

*T*HERE IS NO BEAUTY where there is no object. Without actual physical or sensuous embodiment, even if it be only imagined, the artistic experience does not exist. This at once suggests a contrast with Croce's doctrine. Croce identifies intuition and expression; the latter is as mental as is the former. The artistic experience, he thinks, is purely mental; the actual physical embodiment is a technical matter and serves only the purpose of communication. What is beautiful is the expression and not the work of art. In line with his Hegelianism, he holds that the only reality is living Spirit, immanent and unfolding. The artist not infrequently feels that he has failed to execute his intention. The marble or pigment or phrase does not adequately embody his purpose. From this, Croce argues, it is evident that the artistic feeling or intuition in the sculptor, painter, or poet is greater or deeper than his creation; that the latter is only his attempt to communicate himself. Not so, counters Alexander. Failure to execute his intention in a material medium does not indicate that the artistic expression is purely mental; rather, it is proof that even in imagination it is with marble and pigments and words that the artist is concerned. Failure in expression, when acknowledged, is a confession of failure in experience.

Whatever content there is in the aesthetic experience is in the matter. The artist's work issues not from a completed internal experience, to which the work of art corresponds, but, rather, it proceeds from a passionate excitement about the subject matter.

The poet, like the bird, sings because he must. Just in so far as he has spoken the words, does he possess the imaginative experience embodied in them. The finished object is no translation of his state of mind, for, until he expresses himself, the artist does not know what or how he wants to express. Both are really one: content and medium. Art is like spontaneous humor in this respect: conception and execution go together; for when one is gay, he does not first entertain in image what he wants to say and then find the words in which to say it—the very gaiety itself produces, is, the words. When the artist attempts to paint a portrait, he does not proceed from an imaginative anticipation of the portrait that is to be executed; instead, with passionate interest, he loses himself in the sitter, and the conception and the execution are simultaneous. The hand knows not what the eye sees, nor knows the eye what the hand does, but hand and eye work together.

The story is well known that Leonardo in painting the Last Supper spent, once, three days staring at the convent wall. When told that he was engaged to paint and not stare, he replied that he was doing his work. This is no proof that the idea and the expression are not only distinct but separable. It only shows that the artist with a trained imagination can dispense with the actual laying on of colors: but it is actual colors that he imagines there.

When we analyze the artistic excitement, we find, it is true, first, that it is detained and fixed by the subject-matter, and second, that because of the specific character of the excitement, it is always on the point of expressing itself in the medium. Before the mind will always flit vague ideas of the subject-matter, but this is no proof that idea is independent of matter; for these vague ideas or images are not anticipations of the expression that is ultimately contained in the work of art,—they are, rather, inchoate tendencies to such outward expression, indefinite directions or aspirations which receive definition in the finished work of art: they are the tension of the artistic passion.

Nor, further, does the fact that the artist finds it desirable or urgent to make corrections or change his work, bear out Croce's theory. That theory assumes that the perfect image is in the artist's mind crying for a better expression. But that is not so; for,

if the perfect image were in his mind, he would, except for the
weakness of his technique, have no need to compare his result with
it—he would already have translated his image into fact. The true
explanation for the artist's felt need to correct lies in the fact that
the work fails to give complete satisfaction to the passion which
drives him to outward expression, and so he will alter his work until
satisfaction is reached, until he finds that his passionate artistic
desire is stilled by the product.

The thoughts or feelings, alone, of the artist are, then, insufficient. They must find their expression in the material: it is not
merely useful for communication of his intuitions, but vital to
them, for, without the actual material expression, he would not
have the intuition. Art, then, is not merely material nor merely
mental. In art mind mixes itself with the object; it is the process
whereby the artist takes up material from the real world, such as
clay, sounds, pigments, and by selection makes of them a unity
which embodies the thought or feeling the artist desires to express.

Neither the materials alone, nor the mind alone, would suffice.
The object apart from mind is without value; to become a work of
art it needs must become saturated with our imputations as creators
or spectators. The mere paints or the marble, even when they
issue from the artist's hand, are not in themselves beautiful: they
have beauty only to the eye which mingles its vision with them,
the eye which has the secret of the composition.

The aesthetic value of even a pure tone, one unmixed with
others, derives its purity as a musical value only in a noticed contrast with an impure tone, or in its freedom from admixture.

Regarding a musical composition, it may be said that the tones
harmonize in virtue of certain physical characters they possess,
their vibration, numbers, and, perhaps, in that their partials do not
beat with one another. But the harmony we do not hear. What we
hear are only harmonious tones, and it is the pleasure they give us
distinct from the pleasures appropriate to the separate tones, that
is to say, it is the pleasure of their relational form, which makes us
attribute to them and their physical combination a quality which
we call harmony. It is the composer who makes the rhythm, the
melody, and the harmony; and once composed, it has to be noticed

by the hearer through an aesthetic, a formal, or constructive act with its relevant pleasure. Musical form, just as it needed creation from the composer's mind, needs sustainment from the hearer's mind. Tones do not flow into one another or blend except the mind so hears them. The mere repetition of notes means only that notes occur twice or thrice in a given time; but they mean rhythm when they appeal to the mind or the attention as orderly or rhythmic. The tonal arrangement is harmonious only to an ear which is pleased thereby.

Melody, rhythm, harmony, then, are not in the notes themselves. Mind creates them. A tone may occur thrice in a certain time with equal intervals between the occurrences. These relations are intrinsic, but do not equal rhythm. The order itself is not the rhythm. Harmony has a physical basis in the numbers of tones, but the harmony is a character imputed to the tones so ordered in virtue of the pleasure they excite. So, too, the harmony of colors belongs to them because they please after a certain fashion; and a pure color, like a pure tone, pleases because the mind notes the absence of admixture or contrasts it with mixed colors. So, too, in architecture: the pressure and resistance of the beam and column are physical facts belonging to the stones as ordered. But the grace or ease of the sustainment is an attribution of the aesthetic judgment. Grace does not belong to the column, but is its artistic significance.

This is no less true of the beauty of nature. Nature is beautiful only when seen with the human eye. The imagination selects and combines, and we see nature differently as we are gay or grave, as we add our thoughts or fancies. The beauty of nature is nature passed through our personality. The only important difference between the beauty of nature and that of the fine arts is in the circumstances of the initiation; for the impulsion in natural beauty comes from the thing itself; while in art, the impulsion is from the artist.

"But by what organ do I apprehend this quality of beauty? I can find none. And when we examine each case in turn of natural beauty, always we find, I think, that the beauty depends upon some thought or mood which is imported, I like to say imputed, by the spectators. . . . And so in the end we may agree that no object in nature is beautiful in itself." [1] Nature is beautiful because we select from nature those parts or elements which harmonize.[2]

It is in us, then, that beauty lives, moves, and has its being. The work of art is saturated with our imputations as creators or spectators, and, but for our imputations, it would have no beauty. The mind's imputations do not belong to the object as a physical thing, as do its qualities; they need mind for the generation and sustainment. Nowhere else but in art are Coleridge's verses true:

> *O lady, we receive but what we give,*
> *And in our life alone does nature live.*

II. IS BEAUTY IN THE OBJECT?

In the foregoing exposition we attempted to make it clear that the aesthetic situation is one in which subject and object are in relation. Apart from mind there is no beauty; and we emphasized the role played by mind. In doing this, we think we have been true to our original. Art is mind's product. But from this it does not follow that art is intuition only, and that expression is merely for the purpose of communication. Artistic expression is not for *communication*. It would be truer to say it is for *communion*—mind's communion with material objects. The actual physical expression is the *sine qua non* of all artistic experience. The pen is not used simply to recall words; without an intention to use words for an artistic purpose, the images will not issue. The intuition is not prior to the expression. The intuition develops in the expression, and the expression is generated in the intuition. Although mind plays the major role in the relation, it does not follow that mind alone is important. Stress on its function leads one, naturally, to conclude that beauty is in mind; and from many expressions of his, one might infer that Alexander, too, drew this conclusion. It becomes, therefore, necessary at this juncture to attempt to balance the scales more equally; though it ought to be stated that if frequence of reiteration is indicative of an author's thought, the scales should

1. "The Artistry of Truth," 23 *Hibbert Jour.* 294.
2. "Science and Art," 5 *Jour. Phil. St.* 531.

be let to tip heavily on the side of mind, and beauty allocated there.

In a lecture on *Art and the Material*, delivered in 1925, Alexander speaks of the artist as being both creative and passive. He is creative, e.g., in producing or selecting words or the form of musical sounds. But in all cognition there is the element of discovery, the object being revealed to mind, and this passivity is also to be found in the aesthetic situation. However much the work of art owes its form to the artist, once created it is an expression to be contemplated for its own sake and not merely as a sign, and so reveals to him his own meaning, "and the artistic experience is not so much invention as discovery." [8] This is easier to see in sculpture, as in Michelangelo's unfinished statues of slaves in the Florence Academy. Contemplating them one feels that the artist was involved not so much in making the figures as in chipping off flakes of marble from the figures which were concealed in it and which he laid bare. The discovery was elicited by his own act. Thus one may feel, too, that Shakespeare discovered Hamlet in the English language. With his artistic excitement over the subject of Hamlet's story, and with his insight into Hamlet's imagined nature, he could discover in the English language the selection and combination of words which were fitted to be the expression of his excitement, and in turn they were to surprise him as they surprise us with the imaginations they embody. He says,

> It is true that to make the discovery the gifts of Shakespeare were needed; that is why great artists are rare. But equally the gifts and skill of Newton were needed to discover the law of gravitation in its first form, and other gifts and skill were needed to discover that law in its later and precise form. You cannot discover Hamlet unless you have Shakespeare's mind. But equally unless you have eyes you cannot discover the green trees. Ripeness is all. Except for the features which make the artist's act creative, there is no difference in kind between the discovery of the tree by perception and the discovery of the Slave in the block or of Hamlet in the English language. The

3. Pp. 27–28.

artist's creativeness conceals from us his real passivity. Every artist is in his degree like Shakespeare, who was a reed through which every wind from nature or human affairs blew music.[4]

The passage might be said to be open to various interpretations. It might be said to mean that nature and mind are in affinity, that the former is responsive to artistic expression, that the medium is not abstractly physical, but, as Bosanquet said, "beauty-component," [5] that both participate in a common Spirit, recalling Plato's belief, that it is by the Beautiful that beautiful things are made beautiful. Such a construction of his language is hardly cognate to the spirit of his philosophy. That in artistic expression, the medium is not abstractly physical nor the mind abstractly mental, but both are welded into a unitary kind, Alexander would agree; but from this it does not follow that there is a common Spirit which envelops them, or an Idea in which they participate equally, or that beauty is, as Hegel said, merely the spiritual making itself known sensuously.

Nor do I believe that he meant to indicate the importance of the artist's personality; that art is nature passed through, as Emerson says, the alembic of man, or, as Zola says, the medium of temperament. "You cannot discover Hamlet unless you have Shakespeare's mind," he says. But there is the other side: there must be something the mind can perceive. To see green trees, you need not only eyes, but the green trees. True, in the aesthetic situation there are no green trees until and unless there is mind; but except for this feature, which makes the artist's act creative, *there is no difference in kind*, he says, between the discovery of the tree by perception and the discovery of Hamlet in the English language.

We frankly admit that the language bewilders us. He seems to say that beauty is in the marble or in the words; it is in the wax or in the clay; only, it awaits man to impress or mold or chisel it, or make the selection. But he surely cannot mean this, for there is no beauty except when the material *is formed*, and the form is the artist's contribution. Take away the materials, and, of course, expression becomes impossible. But Alexander seems to want to say

4. P. 29.
5. *Three Lectures on Aesthetics*, 17.

something more. He seems to want to refute Paul that the potter hath power over the clay, of the same lump to make one vessel unto honor and another unto dishonor. He seems to desire to regain an unanimity of the scales by laying an especial stress on the independent nature of the material; but one gathers this intention not from the precise meaning of his words, but rather from their overtones and direction.

In a later expression of his on the question, we find not so much mystery, but more confusion. In a paper on "Beauty and Greatness in Art," [6] he seems to argue that beauty is not a property of a mental state, but rather a property of the work of art itself. It is therein defined as that formal disposition of the physical material in so far as it produces in the mind a special pleasure by the satisfaction of the artistic impulse. It would seem that the status of beauty is not unlike that of a primary quality in the epistemology of Locke. It is a disposition of the physical material which is effective as a *power*. But then he gives an analogy, which is, as will be seen, either misleading or confusing. Sugar has a pleasant taste. But the pleasantness is not in the sugar. It has the quality of sweetness by virtue of which it is pleasant to our taste. We would expect beauty to be like sweetness—but, no. Beauty is like pleasantness in sugar, for it would not be in the work of art except for the mind to which it appeals; "but the form of the material which makes it beautiful corresponds not to the pleasantness of the sugar but to its sweetness."

We must leave the matter thus. We have the expressions (1) that beauty is in the mind, (2) that it is the formal disposition of the physical material; (1) that form is mind's work, (2) that form—like sweetness in sugar—is in the thing itself. We hazard the suggestion that had Alexander adopted our distinction between (1) the genesis and sustainment of beauty in the beauty situation—that there is no beauty apart from the subject-object-in-relation situation, and (2) the location of beauty in that situation—that, given the situation, beauty is a character of the object,—he would have avoided this muddle of inconsistent positions.

6. *Proc. Arist. Soc.*, 1929–30, *vide* p. 211.

III. AESTHETIC FORM AND MEANING

A.[7]

A work of art is the expression of the artistic passion or excitement, and not of any preceding imaginative experience. The experience is generated in and through the expression itself. The artist's meaning is embodied in his very work. The product is not simply a carrier of meaning. It is not merely a medium; if it is in any sense a medium, there is identification of medium and what is meant.

Parallels to this character of the artistic experience are to be found in action; for all knowledge, from bare sensation up to the highest truth, is revealed to our apprehension and through action. The apple is not first apprehended as food and is therefore eaten: we are aware of it as edible in so far as the physical apple excites in us physically the disposition, which is also bodily, to grasp and eat it. Alexander cites the example used by William James of the little boy who, standing too near the edge of the railway platform, rushes in terror from the approaching train: the little boy does not apprehend the train as dangerous and so runs from it, but, forced to run away, he apprehends it thereby as dangerous. "The point is," he says, "that an external quality extorts from us through our susceptibility to it an expressive response, and in that response reveals itself."[8]

The older psychologies assumed that afferent nerves conveyed sensations to the brain and mind, there awakening pictures which represent external things, upon which pictures we then behave appropriately. This is all mythology. What the afferent nerves convey to the brain is nervous excitement. It is efferent or motor reactions, continuous with the afferent processes, in which these excitements discharge, in virtue of which we apprehend the qualities of external things. Objects are revealed to us through these responses only in so far as they stir our senses to react. Broadly, knowledge comes in the first instance through action upon ob-

7. Subsection A is an exposition of Alexander's views. Subsections B and C, *post*, are critical.
8. *Art and the Material*, 20.

jects which themselves by physical and not mental compulsion elicit from us that response. We do not first perceive and then act. We perceive in so far as we act. We know in doing, and knowledge is revelation that comes from practice.

When the body or mind from any internal cause adopts behavior appropriate to a really present object, the object is then said to be presented in idea. Knowledge is present in the mind from past experiences, in ideal form, so that we may be said to know things though they do not act on us presently. But even in the presence of actual things, we know that part of our experience of them is anticipation by way of ideas; they have features which are imputed to them by us. So, too, in act, we impute characters. But the subject of knowing may become emancipated from purely practical interests and no longer change the objects of knowledge. This is what happens in aesthetic appreciation. From practical expression we move on to speculative expression when the normal response is diverted into another path. Instead of acting on the thing, we speak; instead of striking, we hate.

But art, as we have been told, is not simply expression; it is also constructive. Practice is the response directed upon the object to which we respond; construction is productive; and is not directed upon the object which provokes the construction but upon something else. When I strike, I alter the object. When I curse, I make a new object. The artist makes form. What he produces is something different from the thing which wakes the construction.

In poetry, words are detached from their practical uses and used for their own sake lovingly. In practical speech it is otherwise, for therein it is the subject described which interests. The poet's passion is about words and it finds expression in them. He uses them for their own sake, not as external objects to be examined but as the means by which the constructive passion is assuaged.

"Words or other expressive products become the material of art when they are used not for the sake of things which they mean but in themselves and for their own sake." [9] Generally, spoken words are semantic and not aesthetic. A word becomes aesthetic only when it becomes an object and as such is revealed to the

9. *Ibid.*, p. 23.

speaker charged with its meaning. In the aesthetic situation, a word does not simply mean its referent and is then discarded by the mind when the mind is directed upon the thing through it; but the word is held there and becomes itself the thing which occupies the mind, and then it not only has meaning but is fused with the meaning.

"There is no mystery about meaning," he says. "A thing (e.g., a word) *means* the real things or quality or patterns of things for which it stands. But in art the word or marble or drawing has welded into its being the things which it means. Its meaning is part of it in the same way as in the perception of an orange, the round, yellow form does not merely stand for the juiciness of the orange but is actually qualified by and fused with it into one. In the marble block the Hermes does not merely mean life and divinity but is divine and alive, in so far as we appreciate it as a work of art. Its imputations, which come to it from the appreciating mind, and, unlike those of perceived objects, do not belong to it as a physical thing, and, for the appreciating mind, are part of its nature. The artist or the spectator does not ask if the Hermes is really alive; they raise no question of true and false; they see it so. This which is so clear with the statue is true also of language in art. The words are no longer mere sounds, but are alive with the qualities they mean. Paradoxical as it may strike us that a word has taken on in art qualities which it does not possess as mere sound, that is the fact; and when considered it is not stranger than that the dead marble is alive. It may not be single words; it may only be whole phrases, or it may only be the poem as a whole. Certain it is that in the poem the words are new things altered from their common use; enchanting they may be, but they are always enchanted." [10] A line in a poem does not, say, merely describe an old man's grief. For the aesthetic appreciation the grief is actually in the words. (It is to be noted, however, that a poem does not consist of single words, but is a complex unity, and it exhibits unity as an expressive whole, yet each word is fused with its meaning.)

Meanings, then, belong in poetry to the essence of the word, and words are not mere symbols to indicate meanings, as in practical

10. *Ibid.*, p. 24.

speech. A work of art, being an expression, contemplated for its own sake, and not merely as a sign, reveals to the artist his own meaning. Thus, the only subject matter in music is the music itself, its sound form. Its ideas are musical ideas and not emotions. In the plastic arts it is the material as of a certain form which alone is judged aesthetically and is strictly beautiful. Representative art becomes matter for aesthetic judgment only by its form. In the aesthetic appreciation, the form of the work of art is not that of the subject, but the forms of the material used. The architect is an artist not from his practical success in planning a house you can live in, but in so far as he plans the house for its own sake and satisfies him as artist. Beauty lies in the relations of the material of the work of art. These relations are its meaning. The ideas conveyed by beautiful architecture are architectural ideas. Hegel thought the Greek temple to express the finitude of the Greek gods, the Gothic cathedral God's infinitude. This may be true; but the real difference is to be found rather in the flat roof and sustaining columns of the one, and the vaulted roof with high shafts and walls supported by flying buttresses, of the other. Hegel's meaning is the religious rather than the architectural. It is, in every instance, the material formed which is judged aesthetically, and in the aesthetic appreciation subject and form are identical; and form or design, and meaning or significance, are identical.

From this follows as a consequent that a work of art as such cannot be judged from any but the aesthetic viewpoint. You can judge art from the moral point of view only if you take the subject of the work of art as being a translation from something else in the world, an imitation or a criticism of life. But Alexander's position is that the subject of a work of art is nothing other than its form. Even in art that is said to be representative, beauty is in the form; not the form, say, of the sitter, but of the portrait. Subject matter before it enters into art does not at all determine aesthetic value, nor does it determine it thereafter.

But it may happen that the work of art suggests also the subject in the matter proper to the subject and not to the picture. If it does this in a manner so as to overpower or outweigh the formal nature of the subject, it ceases to be beautiful and then lays itself open to moral judgment. So, if the nude is thus treated, that is, with such imperfection of art, that it raises in the spectator ideas or desires appropriate to the material subject, it is false art and bad morals.

But any subject may be beautiful if the artist is artist enough to solve his problem and absorb his subject into his form without the suggestion of qualities which blur the contemplation of form and the introduction of a sensuous appeal. No subject is to be excluded from art if it is treated beautifully, that is, for its form and not for its material enticement. If the artist treats beautifully what we call immoral, it ceases to be immoral. On its material side the subject may be repulsive, yet its form beautiful.

Thus, too, the art of a poem whose substance is nothing, like Peele's dialogue between Paris and Oenone ("Fair and fair and twice so fair"), may be as great as the art of "Lycidas."

This introduces us to the question of degrees of beauty. As is the case of truth and goodness, so, too, of beauty, there are no degrees of value, only of perfection. Beauty is a discernible separate character of works of art. Art is not a criticism of life; Arnold was in error when he refused Omar Khayyam the title of great poetry because he portrays a comparatively low ideal of life. One may, however, maintain that Tennyson is a more perfect artist than Browning. That is a possible comparison; the standard is not beauty but perfection.

When we are concerned with the degree of perfection, the subject matter is content and not form. A work of art may fail of perfection of form, yet you may inquire concerning its degree of perfection, for then the reference is not to the form but to the content. Beauty lies in the relations of the material of the art: in music, in relations of tone; in architecture, in relations of line and enclosed volumes of space and the mechanical stresses of the materials. Perfection lies in the subject matter.

The difference may be illustrated by a contrast of poetry and prose. In prose a subject is put vividly before the mind; in poetry the mind is put within the subject so as to live its life. Poetry is lyrical and dramatic, prose is narrative and chronological. The difference is in kind. The subject plays a more prominent part in prose than in poetry; so the question of degree of perfection or greatness is more easily raised regarding a prose work. Of course in poetry, too, the reader, by the nature of his interest, may select as the subject not the poetic form but a subject extrinsic to the poem itself, and so raise the question of its greatness. If sympathy with the subject as such, even if it be pity and fear in tragedy, prevails over delight in words and their construction, and destroys the equipoise of their sounds and the meanings embodied therein, the result is not poetry but illustration or sentiment. A sharp distinction is to be made between passionate sympathy with the actors in a situation and the proper aesthetic excitement, which is felt in the fitness of the words to express the situation.

The distinction is applicable in the plastic arts and music no less than in letters. If the use of the building obtrudes, it is a prose work; if the use flows from it and is not felt, it is poetic and beautiful. If the painting possesses self-contained life, if it is not its subject which is felt pleasing, but its formal lifeline, color, light and shade,—then it is poetic; if the subject is not felt or conceived in terms of line and color and illumination, but is seen from without, then it is a work of prose. Of course, some prose painting may be higher than poetic painting, as, e.g., Reynolds may be held to be a greater portrait painter than Gainsborough, though the former is prosaic and lacks the grace and charm of the latter's poetic portraits. It is a question not of degrees of beauty but of greatness. Programme music has for its ostensible subject a non-musical idea; yet the tones mean themselves and nothing else. Representation is extrinsic to music as such. Music may proceed from, and suggest, emotion, but it does not exist in order to express it; for it expresses nothing but itself. Think of the representative element, and it is prose, and you can gauge its greatness; think of the musical form, and it is poetry and just beautiful.

B.

If we can speak of the meaning of a work of art—not simply in an honorific sense, as in these lines of Browning's—

> *This world's no blot for us,*
> *Nor blank; it means intensely, and means good;*
> *To find its meaning is my meat and drink,—*

but in a more precise, philosophic sense, we might say, thinking along lines set by Alexander, that beside the systematic and the intensional, there is a third class of meanings, one in which the medium embodies what it would convey; in which content and object are one; resulting in knowledge that is non-mediated. But nothing is gained by speaking of this mental act as one involving meaning; except a possible confusion. It is preferable to characterize it as being intuitive, or an act of bare awareness. Knowledge is always mediated; meaning is always symbolic.

But this is mainly a question of terminology and does not lead to a very fruitful enquiry. Alexander's position is clear. In art there is no transcendent reference. A musical composition "means" only itself; a poem "means" only itself. The creator's mood or emotion or thought is of no account except in so far as it is effective in directing him; and they are absolutely tangential to the auditor's or reader's aesthetic appreciation. Art is pure; it has no commerce with truth or morals. This implies, on the one hand, the inseparability of content and form in the aesthetic experience itself, or, rather, the exclusion of attention or regard for the content; and on the other hand, the separation of content and form in criticism. The former results in the appreciation of beauty, of which there are no degrees; the latter, in the determination of the degree of greatness.

Alexander is not solitary in maintaining the purity of art. It was the *credo* of Oscar Wilde. De Gourmont defended it. He argued that to admit art because it can uplift society or the individual is like admitting the rose because we can abstract from roses a medicine for the eyes. Cubism is a child of the theory. It purifies the sight of things into its essential geometry, and moves in a world of absolute shapeliness, organizing spheres, cubes, and cylinders into architectural units. Hebbel in his *Tagebücher* argues that in the realm of the aesthetic there are no pure or impure subjects, that the highest subject may be contaminated by an ignoble form and the lowliest transmuted by nobility of embodiment. The substance of a work of art is never immoral. If it seems so, it is the fault of the accidental imperfection in the execution of the form. Professor A. C. Bradley, in his *Oxford Lectures on Poetry*, explains what the formula "Poetry for Poetry's sake" means. It means, first, that the experience is an end in itself, is worth having on its own account. And secondly, it means that its *poetic* value is this intrinsic worth alone. He admits that poetry may have also an ulterior value as a means to culture or religion; because it conveys instruction, softens the passions, or furthers a good cause. So much the better, he says. Let poetry be valued for these reasons too. "But its ulterior worth," he adds, "neither is nor can directly determine its poetic worth as a satisfying imaginative experience; and this is to be judged entirely from within. . . . The consideration of ulterior ends whether by the poet in the act of composing or by the reader in the act of experiencing, tends to lower poetic value. It does so because it tends to change the nature of the poetry by taking it out of its own atmosphere. For its nature is to be not a part, nor yet a copy, of the real world, . . . but to be a world of itself, independent, complete, autonomous." [11]

"There is at least one group of privileged people," says Bergson, "who exist in a state of pure perception, that is, in the feeling of things apart from all intellectual concepts, and these are the artists." [12]

"The process of thinking is a sport," says De Gourmont, "although this sport must be free and harmonious. The more it is looked upon as useless, the more one feels the need of making it beautiful. Beauty—that is perhaps its only possible value."

Flaubert in a letter confessed that what seems most beautiful to him, what he most would like to do, would be to write a book without an exterior tie, sustained only by the internal force of its style, a book which would have almost no subject, or, at least, in which the subject would be almost invisible; for, it was his opinion, the most beautiful works are those with the least matter.

Clive Bell, in his essay on Proust, defends the position that the supreme quality in art is formal, by which he means order, sequence, movement and shape. And he adds that "the supreme masterpieces derive their splendour, their supernatural power, not from flashes of insight, nor yet from characterization, nor from

11. P. 5.
12. *La Perception du Changement*, 7.

an understanding of the human heart, even, but from form." [13]
And in another of his books he says, frankly, that "to appreciate
a work of art we need bring with us nothing from life, no knowledge of its ideas and affairs, no familiarity with its emotions." [14]

Alexander would not like to assent that Art for Art's sake means
a divorce of art from life, that art is a world by itself, autonomous
and complete. He would not like to agree with the logic of
Flaubert, De Gourmont, Mr. Bell. In his essay on "Beauty and
Greatness in Art," [15] he says:

> Any subject may be beautiful if the artist is artist enough to
> solve his problem and absorb his subject into his form without
> suggestion of qualities which blur the contemplation of form.
> But it would follow that on the one hand his subject becomes
> thereby defined and limited in isolation from the world to which
> it belongs, and yet, because the artist chooses from the world,
> his art may change not indeed in beauty but in range, and may be
> said to make progress, as it takes in larger and profounder topics
> or enters into them with deeper insight.[16]

He warns that the contrast of beauty and greatness is not to be
exaggerated, for they are not entirely independent of each other;
the profounder and larger the subject, the more difficult to achieve
beauty in it. And he concludes that

> it is easy enough to see that art embodies in its proper material
> of words or other medium the truths which are recognized by
> common experience or discovered by science to be true of
> things or mind. Were it not so, we could hardly understand why
> art appeals . . . to many, or even all, and acquires thus the
> status of objective value.[17]

But we have seen that *sub silentio* he is in sympathy with
Flaubert's wish for a novel about nothing; for he maintains that
a poem of Peele's whose subject is nothing may be judged as
beautiful as Milton's "Lycidas." His denials, in the passages we have

13. *Proust,* 67.   14. *Art,* 25.
15. *Proc. Arist. Soc.,* 1929–30.   16. P. 220.
17. P. 225.

quoted, must be taken as confessions of weakness of premises rather than as compromises of conclusions; for conclusions cannot be compromised; they either do or do not follow from the assumptions. And Bell's and Flaubert's conclusions *do* follow from Alexander's analysis.

Trotsky, in his essay on the Russian Formalist School, in *Literature and Revolt*, argues that the logical conclusion of the formalist idea of art—which regards the process of poetic creation only as a combination of sounds or words, and seeks along this line the solution of all the problems of poetry—is to arm oneself with a dictionary and create, by means of algebraic combinations and permutations of words, all the poetic works of the world! Reasoning "formally," he says, one may produce, e.g., *Eugen Onégin*, in two ways: to do as Pushkin himself did, that is, to subordinate the selection of words to a preconceived artistic idea; or—and from the formalist's viewpoint this latter method is more correct—to solve the problem algebraically, and this means independently of mood, inspiration, or other unsteady things.[18]

Our critic admits that the methods of formal analysis are necessary; but standing alone, they are insufficient. One may count up the alliterations in popular proverbs, classify metaphors, count up the vowels and consonants in a wedding song. The information will enrich our knowledge of folk art, in one way or another;

> but if you don't know the peasant system of sowing, and the life that is based on it, if you don't know the part the scythe plays, and if you have not mastered the meaning of the church calendar to the peasant, of the time when the peasant marries, or when the peasant women give birth, you will have only understood the outer shell of folk art, but the kernel will not have been reached.[19]

So, too, you can establish the architectural scheme of the Cologne cathedral by measuring the base and the height of its arches, by determining the three dimensions and the placement of the columns, etc. But if you are ignorant of the character of a mediaeval city, of the Catholic Church, of the Middle Ages, you will never

18. P. 172.   19. P. 180.

understand the Cologne cathedral. "The effort to set art free from life, to declare it a craft self-sufficient unto itself, devitalizes and kills art. The very need of such an operation is an unmistakable symptom of intellectual decline." [20]

Consider, e.g., Mr. Eliot's preference for Dryden as critic to Aristotle and Coleridge. The latter two are historical or philosophical critics, while Dryden was a "literary critic," a purist. Aristotle and Coleridge are rejected because to both art is a means to a better, and more significant life, because the reference to life pervades the whole of their criticism. But the least of the company is made the corner-stone of the critic's mansion, because his only tools were mere mechanical rules about certain unities, because he took Aristotle and pumped the life blood out of his veins. Dryden's purity is his sterility. The impurity of Aristotle and Coleridge is their virility.

To divorce art from life, to substitute art for life, is to provide an undeniable reason why a man of brawn and brain should renounce art forever.

Formalism in art ultimately means its reduction to mathematics; the exclusion of all beauty but the cold, austere, pure, perfect beauty of number. Euclid alone has looked upon beauty bare, says Miss Millay; and Roy Campbell sings of the arrival of the clear anatomy with winter, "the paragon of art, that kills all forms of life and feeling, save what is pure and will survive." It is the Pythagorean celebration of number, the Spinozistic "reduction" of all reality to the order of geometry.

But the great creators of art are the first to disclaim any theory which explains their creativity as passionless. If a man does not create with his blood and muscle, and suffer birth- and death-pangs in so doing, if his expression does not issue from deep experience, then his work is still-born, and should be shunned. "Why do I write? What I have in my heart must come out," says Beethoven, "and that is why I compose." [21] In the first allegro of his Symphony No. 5, in C minor, says Berlioz, Beethoven revealed all the secrets of his being—"his most private griefs, his fiercest wrath, his most

20. P. 181.   21. Rolland, *Beethoven*, p. 102.

lonely and desolate meditations, his midnight visions, his bursts of enthusiasm." [22]

Wagner, writing to Liszt in 1854, said:

As I have never in my life enjoyed the true felicity of love, I shall erect to this most beautiful of my dreams a monument in which, from beginning to end, this love shall find fullest gratification. I have sketched in my head a "Tristan and Isolde," the simplest of musical conceptions, but full blooded. With the "black flag" which waves at the end, I shall then cover myself, to die.

Schumann wrote to a colleague regarding his Symphony No. 1, in B flat:

Could you infuse into your orchestra in the performance a sort of longing for the Spring, which I had chiefly in mind when I wrote in February 1841? The first entrance of trumpets, this I should like to have sounded as though it were from high above, like unto a call to awakening.

Rodin thinks that in representing the universe as he imagines it, the artist formulates his own dreams, celebrates his own soul.

Tschaikovsky's love for Nadejda von Meck; Keats's passion for Fanny Brawne; Goethe's multitudinous love affairs—one mentions these instances not as proofs but as illustrations: illustrations of the thesis that it is no more possible to separate beauty and greatness, form and content, than it is to abstract Beethoven the musician from Beethoven the man; and where nature has not made the separation, we cannot.

Bergson's claim of privilege may well rouse our suspicions. All claims of privilege are suspicious. In art, the claim leads to preciousness. Art for Art's sake means snobbishness. It means retirement to an ivory tower; a lifting of the skirts out of the dust of the mart; indifference to the claims and needs of society; cultivation of art as a substitute for responsible living; an escape to the children's playroom. It issues out of a feeling of frustration, a sense of the uselessness of social endeavor, or the fear that it might be de-

22. Quoted by Grove, *Beethoven and His Nine Symphonies*, 152.

manded that one give an account of himself in the broad daylight.

It ought to be mentioned, also, that the inviolability of art cannot be attained by considering it "pure"; for such consideration introduces the double standard in criticism. And so, what cannot be condemned as inartistic may be condemned as immoral or impolitic.

And a double standard is as vulgar in criticism as it is in household morality. It leads to hypocrisy, unsteadiness, and, ultimately, to the indifference of insensibility. What a sorry spectacle, e.g., the late Mr. Saintsbury presented. In his morals, he was reactionary; in his art criticism, he tried to have the impartiality of the purist. So, as a devout believer, he deplored Matthew Arnold's disbelief in miracles; and yet he averred to relish greatly the poems of Arnold which have their source in his disbelief. He applauded complacently Zola's picture of the "grime and glare and scorch of the furnaces" and "the thirst and lust and struggles of their slaves,"—and yet objected to a freeing of the slaves as "robbery." [23]

Alexander maintains that a work of art is to be appreciated for its formal qualities only; to enjoy it for any other character is not to enjoy it as a work of art but as another object. This point can be quite pleasantly turned about, and one can say that to enjoy art for its formal qualities is not to enjoy it as art but as an abstraction or as a geometrical object; just as to enjoy it for its religious quality is to enjoy it as a religious object. The point is this: that the formalist is himself guilty of the very act of which he accuses others; for he, too, does not appreciate the work of art as an entirety, for its many-faceted aspects, but only for one of its characters; namely, its formal configuration.

C.

Formalism is rejected because it is an attenuation; because it substitutes for the appreciation of a whole a bare mathematical abstraction; because it does not enrich experience, but substitutes art for living; because it is founded on a sharp separation of form from content; because it introduces the double standard in art appreciation and criticism.

23. Cf. editorial in *New Republic*, Feb. 8, 1933.

On the other hand, art is not *mere* representation. When we hate with Iago, tremble with Desdemona, die with Tess, experience peace and plenty with Innes, suffer with Tschaikovsky, we experience genuine organic emotions; but if we experience only them, our experience is not aesthetic. Other people get the same or similar experiences from drinking wine, or the celebration of mysteries, or the cultivation of love. Emile Faguet has said that the pleasure which the reader finds in tragedy is malicious. That may or may not be; certainly, however, greater regard must be had for the man who himself lives through the experiences than for the one in the concert hall or theatre who "lives" through them in a vicarious fashion. Again, art is a substitute for life; and any substitute, because it is only that, is colorless, tawdry, cheap.

Representation is guilty of those very vices of which it accuses formalism. If the latter disregards content, the former disregards the formal element. It, too, appreciates only an abstraction. For the formal rules of art, it substitutes a moral or psychological test, and recognizes, also, the double standard.

Thus in all criticism an impasse is reached, one house wishing a plague on the other. All this is, I think, due to a faulty analysis of the nature or place of meaning in the aesthetic situation. We think of words having meanings; also musical sounds, bodily gestures, spatial configurations. This leads us to view art as a language, or a method which uses for communication languages we understand. The formalist, on the other hand, feels that if art only communicates thoughts, emotions, feelings, etc., then it does not convey a meaning that is *sui generis*, or evoke an excitement that is recognizably and unmistakably aesthetic.

But it seems not to have been noticed that while a sound may mean a thing, *a thing may mean a sound.* And here we touch upon the distinguishing feature of art. *In the aesthetic experience, instead of language meaning the material of experience—things, ideas, emotions, feelings,—this material means language.*

Let us illustrate. It is known that the famous phrase of four unison notes which opens the first movement of Beethoven's Fifth Symphony was suggested to the composer by the note of the yellow-hammer as he walked in the park in Vienna, and that he has spoken of these notes that "*so pocht das Schicksal an die Pforte.*" The note of the bird suggests, means, to contemplative Beethoven, Fate knocking on the door. One does not need to be a musical genius to link up a bird call with a philosophic thought. As Santayana has said, every kitchen-maid is a philosopher, for doesn't she know that beneath the peel is the edible potato? that surface *means* substance? But Beethoven's musical genius comes into play when Fate's knock he takes to mean those four unison notes with which the Symphony opens. There is translation, but not the kind we indulge in when we read newspapers, or talk shop, or stop at a traffic signal. The artist translates the things which are usually *meant* into the things which usually *mean*.

In the workaday life a facial expression is taken to mean a psychical state. But to the actor the process is reversed. A feeling to him means a facial expression. He may experience the proper feeling, but if he cannot "register" it, he is a failure. Indeed, if he can register the feeling without really suffering it internally, well and good; neither the director nor the audience cares about that. To the dancer, her emotions or conceptions mean bodily gestures —precisely the reverse of what takes place, say, in a medical diagnosis. The poet hears the trot of horses on the road and the nimble walk of a dog. But to her these sounds mean two lines of poetry:

> '*Tis the rhythmic beat of a horse's feet*
> *And the pattering paws of a sheep-dog bitch.*

Now the spectator or auditor reverses the process, *but only provisionally*. The prelude *L'Après-midi d'un faune* presents an illustration of Mallarmé's poems, and the music evokes the scenes in which the faun's longings and desires pass in the heat of an afternoon. In Ravel's *Daphnis et Chloé* he hears the murmur of rivulets, songs of birds, sees the dawn break, etc. In Beethoven's Symphony he hears Fate's knock. In every gesture of the actor's, in every movement of the dancer's, in every line of the painting, in every verse of the poem, he discovers a meaning. Art is communicative, it is expressive, or, if you prefer, evocative. Art is representative to the auditor or spectator.

But it is something else, too. The work of art not only *means*, but is *meant*. The appreciator is also the creator. The latter has a feeling or an emotion or a thought which he shapes into an artistic form by means of words or paints or sounds. *His mental content means the work of art and is in turn meant by it.* The appreciator participates in the same process. He may feel that the work of art means the emotion he experiences, the mood it induces, the thought it conveys, *but at the same time he feels that his mood means the musical composition or the poem. The aesthetic experience is the whole transaction between himself and the object, and the commerce between them is, as it were, on a two-way thoroughfare.* Make the meaning in the aesthetic situation a one-way direction, from object to mind, and the result is representative art; from mind to object, and the result is formal art. Meaning in art is like the ladder in Jacob's dream; angels go up on the rungs from earth to heaven, and angels go down on the rungs from heaven to earth.

In art, then, we do not find the identification of medium and meaning. Indeed, there is no absolute medium; for words and sounds are in the creative act the things that are meant and not the carriers of meaning, and at the same time the carriers and not the burden of meaning.

Swinburne is probably the best example in English verse of the sorry failure of a great poet. The fluency of his later poems impresses us as superfluity, his song a mere sing-song, his fire only a column of smoke, his eloquence mere declamation. What has happened? we wonder. The explanation is probably that from Eton and Balliol he moved into a world of words, and in them he lived and moved. There was no intercourse between a great soul and great words; the world of the latter was complete, independent, autonomous: "in the beginning was the word."

In Donne we experience the difficulty of now living in a world of sounds and now in a world of meanings, a strain between the ear hearing and the intellect overhearing; sound and meaning living on speaking terms, but not flesh of one flesh and bone of one bone.

Next to the evil of living in a realm of words exclusively, is the evil of keeping sound and sense separated. Like Castor and Pollux, they should be distinguishable but inseparable.

What Heine has said of Goethe's lyrics is true of all great art. "*Die harmonischen Verse umschlingen dein Herz wie eine zärtliche Geliebte, das Wort umarmt dich, während der Gedanke dich küsst.*" Great art is like a river: the living waters rush freely within a form that confines. Empty the channel of the waters, and what remains will interest only the student of rocks and soils. D. H. Lawrence, in his essay on "Sex versus Loveliness," remarks that no one can be quite so repellently ugly as a really pretty woman. "When the sex-glow is missing, and she moves in ugly coldness, how hideous she seems, and all the worse for her externals of prettiness." I do not agree with him that beauty is a matter of experience exclusively, and not at all of concrete form. But I do agree that the form without the experience results in "a nasty, clayey creature whom everybody wants to avoid." There can be no poetry unless the stuff of poetry gets into it, unless it contains the deeps out of which it must issue.

On analysis it may be seen that a work of art has a double meaning: it means a particular and also a universal. In the aesthetic, as in all meaning situations, there is the fusion of a percept and a concept. Except when we suffer a mental state that is characterized by a blank stare and a gaping, adenoid mouth, every least presentation brings to us a concept and a percept. We are not, of course, always conscious of the conceptual element; its place may seem to be taken by a feeling. But on analysis its presence is always discovered. Knowledge always reveals a structure, and such revelation is mediated by a concept. Sensations are never pure. Kant's dictum, that percepts without concepts are blind and concepts without percepts are empty, is a truth specially prominent in the field of aesthetics.

Our meaning may be brought home by a comparison of two American poets, Robert Frost and Edwin Arlington Robinson. Amy Lowell has characterized the poetry of Robinson as "universal" and that of Frost as "particular." This distinction is not an invidious one, although we would give to the terms a meaning other than that intended by her. She doubtlessly had in mind that discrimination between history and poetry made by Aristotle; so that the prize would necessarily belong to Robinson. But to us both poets are particular and both are universal, with this difference, however:—adapting an expression of Goethe's—Robinson uses the particular for the sake of the universal, while Frost discovers the universal in the particular.

Robinson is dantesque in his method: his characters are not personalities, self-sufficient, but representative and exemplifying, allegoric. Cassandra, e.g., is like Rabbi Ben Ezra, a disembodied spirit, a mouthpiece, a voice behind a veil. The Mother in "The Gift of God" is not your mother or mine, but motherhood in general, a surrogate for the Platonic Idea of Mother. So, too, Flammonde, the Man-Against-the-Sky, John Evereldown: they are not men, but qualities, traits, vices or virtues. Robinson's characters are those of an allegorist. The poet gives to them a name, but not a local habitation. And so they remain airy nothings.

Frost, on the contrary, expresses what is particular without regard for, or reference to, what is universal, of whose nature it partakes: yet—and this is the marvel—he so delineates and expresses it that it takes about itself an aura; it becomes more than itself: it is a fact and also a truth, temporal and yet eternal, a person and yet a type. Frost has the method which Keats counseled Shelley to adopt and which is beautifully evidenced in the "Ode on a Grecian Urn"; that by which the elusive becomes concrete, the diffused becomes quintessential. He does not make the flower in the crannied wall tell the story of Man or Earth, but in portraying the flower he does his work so that in the result we find the intrinsic being of these. Its speech, however, cannot be heard; it must be overheard. He draws the part as though it were the whole; and yet unostentatiously, and only by a language of gesture, is the part made to express the whole.

Hugo has said of Cellini that he could create a lily that, becoming a woman, still remains a lily. All great art does just this. It draws, as Emerson has said—it draws together the poles of the universe. The greatness of art, its power, its appeal—its universality—lies in its concreteness. The artist creates a particular without thought or suggestion of the universal. But whoever learns the meaning of this particular grasps also the universal with it. The two are inseparable. But it must be emphasized that, except in allegoric art, the particular is not used for the sake of, or because it means, the universal. The latter does not obtrude. Like personality, it does not force itself upon you; frequently, it comes embodied in humbleness and gentility; it is only after long friendship, or arduous wooing, that you discover this meaning of the person. You may feel the presence at once; but it is an obnoxious personality that flauntingly thrusts itself on your attention. "Lift the rock and there you will find me, cleave the wood and there I am." It is something felt, but not seen; learned, but not presented.

These meanings are not always fixed. Indeed, it may be that in music it happens rarely that the same particular or perceptual meaning is conveyed to several auditors. How many people would agree, e.g., that Rimsky-Korsakov's composition portrays the flight of the bumblebee, if they were not told its title?

Professor Weld's survey of introspective reports reveals an enormous individual variation in the mental contents of the several auditors who were his subjects.[24] He played Voelker's "Hunt in the Black Forest," obviously a descriptive piece, but the title was not disclosed. One described the composition as a portrayal of a battle; another, of a circus; a melodrama; a hunting scene. Even purely mimetic descriptions, such as the barking of dogs, wholly failed to suggest situations such as the composer had hoped to simulate. The conclusion is that the composer is almost entirely powerless to evoke any one mental picture in the minds of all his auditors.

It may be that in music (probably dancing, too) the particular meaning plays an incidental role; but it is undeniably prominent in the other arts, plastic and literary. Indeed, as we have said, the artist's achievement is tested, in part, by his failure or success in conveying a particular meaning through a sensuous or material embodiment.

24. "Experimental Study of Musical Enjoyment," 23 *Amer. J. Psych.*, 245–308.

Nor can it be said that there is usually agreement on the universal meaning. What is the meaning of the "Mona Lisa"? It is as little likely that two random spectators will agree on its meaning as on the meaning of God. So, too, of *Hamlet*, the "Ode to the West Wind," etc. Wagner's thought was that Beethoven's Seventh Symphony represents the apotheosis of the dance; Marx heard in it a tale of Moorish knighthood; Oulibischeff thought it pictured a masquerade!

But failure to agree on the meaning does not disprove the existence of some one meaning in each spectator or auditor, or many such meanings. Goethe has said of one of his own works that it contains more than he had put into it. That is true of all great art. The maker of telescopes must use the instrument which is the product of his own handiwork if he would see stars in the heavens which escape detection by the naked human eye. So, too, the poet, like Goethe, or the musician, like Beethoven, may use his own works when he, like us, seeks revelation of the arcana of the universe, those diffused essences subterranean, ethereal, and sub-auditory: those disclosures which, in our prosy way, we call universal meanings, without which a work of art—a drama, portrait, symphony—would be the bare imitation of a natural thing or event, differing from a child's three-line drawing of a cow only in its more consummate technique; without which it could not happen that nature, as Oscar Wilde has said, imitates art: that we see an English countryside through the eyes of Gainsborough or Constable, Wessex through the temperament of Hardy, the sea through the mind of Conrad or Masefield, the *lacrimae rerum* through Tschaikovsky or Sibelius, and death through the alembic of Wagner.

CHAPTER 6

Goodness

I. COHERENCE THEORY OF GOODNESS

*M*ORAL GOODNESS is distinctively human, belongs to conduct as it issues from will and is social." [1] This passage introduces us at once to the leading notions in Alexander's moral theory: (1) that morality is an affair of motives or will, and (2) that it is in essence social.

It has been supposed that goodness belongs to the will in itself as a mere mental function. But this is erroneous. The will which is the subject-matter of the science of ethics is not the isolated will, but the will in its inter-relation with other wills. And the will becomes the subject of moral judgment because of its concern with objects which exist apart from it and are contemplated by minds in common.

> Minds can judge each other as good or bad only as directed upon these objects. I can judge you to be doing right or wrong only so far as I see you willing an object which I approve or condemn. It is not your will I approve merely as a mental process; what I approve is your will for temperate drinking or preservation of property. There is no such thing as inner morality, if it is thought of as independent of what is willed. [2]

Goodness, then, like beauty, is an amalgam of mental and non-mental existence. It is a new reality, and, as we shall see, the goodness of this new reality is its internal coherence.

1. *Space, Time, and Deity*, II, 273.   2. II, 279.

But the role played by the non-mental object is not to be stressed. While human satisfactions must take account of such an object, and of the laws of external and of human nature, their goodness is determined by no quality they possess, but by how far they satisfy persons and are approved by them.

While all action is, admittedly, response to environment, the more important part of that environment in social or moral action is our fellow-men. Not only do we take account of their approbations and disapprobations, but they are themselves the objects of our appetites. It is consideration of their wants and opinions that results in a system of moral principles. "Accordingly it is indifferent to say that morality is the adaptation of human action to the environment under social conditions, or that it is the system of actions approved by man under the conditions set by the environment." [3]

Morality results from our attempt to satisfy our affections and desires, some of which are sympathetic or natural affections for others, and some of which are dissympathetic or self-regarding. The good wills are those which cohere with each other; the bad wills are those which fail to fall into the system of cohering wills, and are, therefore, excluded. The good acts are those which are coherent, the bad acts are those which are incoherent.

Before the system of coherent wills is constituted, the individual wills have wants and prefer claims, and the wills clash one with the other. In the system, the claims, so far as their satisfactions can be admitted, consistently with the claims of other members, are approved, become rights, and their performance an obligation. The good act is that which is approved as pleasing the collective wills and not merely the individual's own will.

And this act may vary according to the nature of the individual and the place he holds in society. But this does not mean that there is no universal element in morality. So far as the act is allowed, it is approved for anyone in those circumstances and of that nature and temperament, and the approval of other wills belongs to the act not as a favor to the individual, but to any such person under such conditions.

3. II, 274.

There are moral goods, just as there are moral wills. For the wills that are approved as good or disapproved as bad, are, as we have said, wills for certain objects, and the wills are judged along with the objects. The object willed is a fact in the external world, or an internal enjoyment. (In the latter instance, the fact, such as the suppression of an illegitimate thought, is not, strictly, an object, but the contents of the will.)

The external objects willed take the form of propositions; such as, This food is eaten, This property is distributed among certain individuals. The sum of such propositions constitutes the conditions by which moral institutions are maintained. The individuals will the external facts, and the consummation of the acts of will is the satisfactions of the individuals. An individual does not will another's happiness, but only the conditions which, when realized, secure it. The satisfactions are moral goods. The objects secured by willing are not in themselves good or bad but only in so far as they supply such satisfactions, in ways approved by the collective sanction.

> The good is thus a system of satisfactions of persons which is effected by right willing. Mere satisfactions, such as possession of wealth, or pleasure, or, in general, happiness, . . . are not of themselves good in the moral sense. . . . What makes them morally good is that these satisfactions of persons should be organised and made coherent within the individual, and the relation of individuals to one another within the social group, and thus "maximised" or made as great as possible consistently with the conditions of social life.[4]

Goodness, then, does not reside in the bare satisfaction alone, or in the will alone, but in the union of satisfying objects with the wills which sustain them; i.e., it belongs to the moral institutions themselves which are made by collective men. Individuals are good who act in the spirit of the institutions, and the institutions are good as securing coherently the satisfactions of the wills of the individuals.

There is not, of course, an antecedent coherence in the non-

4. II, 277.

mental reality, in the case of the good. That is brought about by the wills themselves, though in obedience to the conditions imposed by the nature of things. The good institutions, which enter into the system, are a human creation, by which men adapt themselves to their non-mental environment.

It appears, then, that the problem of morality is to secure a coherent distribution of satisfactions among persons. Evil, then, needs to be defined as misdistribution.

> Drinking wine is not in itself evil. What is evil is the intemperance. The passion is gratified to the full. This may be legitimate in the case of certain affections, but it is not legitimate in this case when the full extent of the passion is for more wine than is consistent with the man's own health and work or his intercourse with others. A private person who demands my purse is a thief and bad, but the Chancellor of the Exchequer may demand it legitimately if he has the sanction of Parliament.[5]

Two things more remain to be mentioned. (1) The moral character, in its contrast with the immoral one, is an instance of the contrast established within the organic world generally between the successful type and the individuals which conform to it. Moral disapproval is the process by which the unsocial type is discarded in human life. Moral good, then, is a type of life which is engaged in the same struggle with the evil type as appears in the organic world in general.[6]

(2) There are degrees in perfection of moral life, just as there are degrees in perfection of animal types, but there are no degrees of goodness. While the goodness of one age may be inferior to that of another age, to be good is to be good, and what is good

5. II, 280–1.
6. Cf. the bio-sociological theory of law, founded also on the idea of selection. Law results from the conflict or competition of legal institutions or of legal doctrines, from which those emerge which are most adapted to further the progress of the race. Law, then, is an aggregate of the means by which a group protects itself against hindrances to its continuance or to its progress found in the actions of certain of its members or in the hostility of other groups. See Roscoe Pound, "Scope and Purpose of Sociological Jurisprudence," 25 *Harvard L. Rev.* 498–9. See his criticism of the theory on p. 503. Discussion of this biological theory of morals is to be found throughout *Moral Order and Progress*.

once remains good for the circumstances under which it was good. Goodness may acquire a fuller reality, but no greater reality.

II. TWO FORMS OF THEORY DISTINGUISHED

The essence of morality, then, is coherence. Coherence of what? Is goodness the "quality" (1) of an individual whose impulses cohere with one another, within himself, or (2) of an individual whose will coheres with the other wills who constitute his society, or of society which allows a maximization of coherence within an individual by offering the conditions which make that possible, together with a similar maximization within every other individual?

Our exposition does not offer a clear answer, and its absence is fatal to Alexander's moral views. Let us see what is to be found in Alexander's writings that may dispel ambiguity on this point.

(1) The problem of morality he defines as the securing of a coherent distribution of satisfactions among persons.[7] And evil is defined as misdistribution.[8] Immediately following these definitions, Alexander instances the drinking man, and says that the intemperate gratifications of this passion is illegitimate "when the full extent of the passion is for more wine than is consistent with the man's own health and work *or* his intercourse with others." He adds that the Greeks were right when they identified justice with virtue as a whole. "For the essence of justice is in distribution; and all badness is injustice either to oneself or others or both." [9]

In an earlier passage he says that

what makes them morally good is that these satisfactions of persons should be organised and made coherent *within the individual, and in the relation of individuals to one another within the social group*, and thus "maximised" or made as great as possible consistently with the conditions of social life.[10]

(2) He defines goodness as "the kind of conduct, or the kind of satisfaction secured by conduct, which can cohere with the claims of other persons." [11]

7. II, 280.

8. *Ibid.*

9. II, 281. Italics supplied.

10. II, 277. Italics supplied.

11. II, 280.

In two passages he seems to be aware of the possibility of there being a conflict between the claims of satisfactions on the ground of individual coherence and the claims of another group of satisfactions on the ground of social coherence; and he attempts a resolution.

In the first passage [12] he says that "morality approves both sets of claims in their measure. It may even be a failure of duty for an artist to devote himself to philanthropy, but it is moral judgment itself which sanctions this preference." Whose preference does he mean, that of the individual or of society? There can be no doubt that he means the latter. For, he adds, morality "counts the gifts of a man as material which he can contribute to the common good, and decides how far he is to use those gifts, and in what proportion to the other claims which it also sanctions." And, he continues, the individual must learn the difficult lesson of finding more pleasure in following the right than he loses from the sacrifice of his desires; for he must recognize the fact that he has no rights inherent in himself. He has claims; his rights are the claims which the group sanctions. Obviously, what Alexander means in this passage by morality is the social impulse. Where, then, is the resolution, if one impulse is given preference over another? If the social impulse silences and chains the selfish impulse? There is a peace attained, but it is a peace in which one combatant is victor and the other captive. It is not the peace of coherence but of conquest.

But this need not be so if the social impulse is judged to be the wider one; so that its precedence would not mean the suppression or annihilation of the selfish impulse but the incorporation of the latter. And this Alexander seems to suggest in a passage in the chapter on "Freedom." [13] Experience shows us, he says, that complete determination of the personality on all its sides is more attainable in the good man than the bad one.

> For goodness is essentially the balanced development of all sides of human nature, its personal and its social elements all included; and though the bad man may exhibit a high degree of organization under some mastering impulse, he in general leaves certain

12. II, 282–3.   13. II, 320.

sides of his nature undeveloped or else is wanting in certain
necessary elements of character.[14]

NOTE

In *Moral Order and Progress* [15] there appear both forms of the
theory, with an emphasis on the latter. Good in the individual is
defined as an equilibrium of functions. His act is good which is
required by his past and future needs, taken as he is with all his
faculties. It implies an order or system of acts which are regulated
by reference to each other. "The good life as a whole is a system
of conscious acts, where each function has its limits prescribed to
it by the demands of all other functions, so that no faculty shall
perform its functions to the detriment of another." [16] The good
character consists of various conscious acts, which, by their inter-
connections, present a man as embodying a law or plan, whatever
that plan may be. Morality establishes a balance between a man's
various feelings, love, hunger, anger, etc. Every man is good in
so far as his acts conform to this adjustment.

Yet, "no act is regarded as good which does not at once satisfy
the agent's position in the whole, and maintain a certain relation
between him and others, which secures them a like freedom in their
work." [17] Good conduct must fulfill two conditions; namely, it
must secure the wants on part of the person performing it, but
these must be such as are compatible with similarly recognized
wants in others. "What morality requires is that each person should
find his place in a manner compatible with the same claims on the
part of all,—the highest specialisation being identical with the
completest unity. It thus involves an equilibrium between the mem-

14. In his subsequent writings it seems that the notion of coherence in the
second sense, as above described, is what Alexander means. In the article on
"Truth, Goodness, and Beauty," in 28 *Hibbert Jour.*, 616, 1930, he says that
the moral sense is the satisfaction of the social impulse. "Virtue is what
satisfies the social sense, the substance of morality can only be discovered by
discovering experimentally what unites the members of society into a common understanding." In the article on "Morality as an Art," 3 *Jour. Phil.
St.*, 143, 1928, he says that not utility is the test but the possibility of others
to attune their impulses to my act. Morality is the harmony of individual
wills as engaged in society.

15. Bk. II, ch. 2.   16. P. 99.   17. P. 114.

bers of the society,—an order or system in which the functions of each are maintained." [18] Morality establishes a system of relations between the members of a society, by each of which relations the individuals are directed to their respective places in the system, while the good act forms the bond of connection between them. Good conduct falls within the social order; bad conduct is that which fails to adjust itself and is condemned.

Alexander recognizes that the two tests may clash. In the one case an act is good which is adjusted to an organization of the individual's activities; in the other, an act is good in which the agent is adjusted to an order of persons, the adjustment implying in both cases that every other member of the order is satisfied at the same time in the measure possible under the conditions. He thinks, however, that there is an identity of principle between the two orders. I have difficulty in following him on this point, but I gather he means that the individual ideal functions in, and is circumscribed by, the social ideal. A man's wants, even those which are seemingly self-regarding, have a social character. In harmonizing himself, then, he must not break the social equilibrium. The system that prevails between a man's activities when he is considered alone is an expression of that individual place he holds in the moral society in virtue of which he forms a center of repellent and attractive relations. Equilibrium within the individual means adjustment to his environment, but there is one part of the environment with which he has a special relation; namely, the members of his society. Equilibrium within the individual means adjustment to the social environment.

The adaptation of man to his environment means in fact an adjustment by which the conflicting interests of various individuals in a society are reconciled. Morality means a system of conduct in which good persons acquiesce. The adjustment means the creation of a certain type of character, all such characters acquiescing in one another's free development, and conversely those lines of conduct are considered free development in which the other characters can acquiesce. [19]

What does it all come down to? It seems to us it all reduces itself

18. P. 117.   19. P. 275.

to Plato's ideal of specialization of function and specialization of virtue, and all talk of harmony in the individual is sheer gibberish. The "free development" in which the other characters can acquiesce may mean the "free development" of a soldier or of a cobbler or of a philosopher-king. The social equilibrium is not the sum of the individual equilibria of A, B, C, etc., for the character of the individual equilibrium is dependent upon the sufferance of society. It therefore follows that society may be an organization of warped individuals. At any rate, it seems nonsensical to speak of the harmony or equilibrium of the individual when one means something else.

III. PRESUPPOSITIONS OF THE THEORY

Professor Alexander does not *argue* that coherence, in either of the senses, constitutes goodness or morality. He *asserts* it. But the argument need not really be formulated: it is quite obvious that coherence is morality because its purpose is to maximize satisfactions, and the satisfaction of a desire or an impulse is always good. This is the thread of thought that runs throughout his discussion, is the underlying motif. The proposition that satisfaction of desire is essentially or unquestionably good; and its consequent that the more desires satisfied, the "better"—are the basis for the coherence theory of goodness.

This is largely implicit in Alexander. It is explicit in other philosophers who are in essential agreement with him. Let us consider several.

A. To Professor Holt, as a man thinketh in his heart, so is he; and man's heart, so to speak, is full of "wishes." The wish includes desire, tendency, impulse, purpose. It is "a course of action which some mechanism of the body is *set* to carry out, whether it actually does so or not." [20] It is something which the body can do, a course of action with reference to the environment which the body can carry out; [21] a course of action which the body executes or is prepared to execute with regard to some object or some fact of its environment. [22] Thought is the motor attitude prepared, and will

20. *The Freudian Wish*, pp. 3–4. 21. P. 48.
22. Pp. 56–7.

is the motor touched off. He agrees with Spinoza that will and intellect are one and the same, and with James that beliefs are rules of action, and the function of thinking is but one step in the production of active habits.

"Even two reflexes," he says, "acting within one organism bring it about that the organism's behavior is no longer describable in terms of the immediate sensory stimulus, but as a function of objects and of situations in the environment"; [23] *and mind is only integrated reflex behavior.*[24]

The prophetic nature of thought is due to the fact that it is a preceding labile interplay of motor settings with too small energy to produce overt bodily movements.[25] Thought is a latent course of action with regard to the environment.

Will, then, and thought and object are in inseparable conjunction. From this psychological basis, Holt would construct a *Real-ethik*, building *von unten hinauf*, rather than *von oben herab*. The end of the Good Life is the integration of wishes, avoiding dissociation and suppression. Moral conduct is discriminating conduct; morality is wisdom; right is conduct attained through discrimination of facts fulfilling all of man's wishes at once, suppressing none. The motion of life is forward, the motive power is from behind—from the wishes. Instead of suppressing wishes, discriminate the facts; for suppression is due to lack of knowledge; mental doubt and volitional indecision are inseparable and due to ignorance. Truth, then, is the sole moral sanction, and ethics is, as Epictetus said, dealing wisely with the phenomena of existence.[26]

B. In Mr. Joad's *Common-Sense Ethics* the social implications of the coherence theory, likewise founded on an analysis of impulses, appear more clearly than in Holt's book.

The most important factor in the individual's constitution is impulse. It is impulse that expresses his individuality; that constitutes the peculiar essence of his personality. It is his principle of growth, and the source of his progress. It is, in fact, the very expression of his life.

That the individual may live a full life, it is necessary that his

23. P. 80.   24. P. 82.
25. P. 95.   26. Pp. 125, 130-2, 141, 147-8.

impulses have free scope for expansion and development. For only by following his impulses can he develop his full nature and realize himself.

Thwarting or suppressing impulses has two dire consequences: (1) there is a general reduction in the individual's vitality, resulting in boredom and lack of interest, and a warfare within the individual; and (2) thwarted impulses are driven underground and form the repressed complexes and perversions, with which we have become acquainted through the writings of psychoanalysts.

But it must be noted that there are in the main two classes of impulses: (1) the class of creative impulses, and (2) the class of possessive impulses. Mr. Joad's theory is not one which tells us that all impulses are to be encouraged and indulged merely because they are impulses. Only the creative impulses are to be encouraged, and at the expense of the others. For the creative impulses can be indulged to an unlimited extent without interfering with the impulses of others.[27]

C. Mr. I. A. Richards has a cognate theory. His position is that anything is valuable which will satisfy an appetency without involving the frustration of some equal or more important appetency; that is to say, the only reason for not satisfying a desire is that thereby more important desires will be thwarted. Morals are thus purely prudential, expedient. The importance of an impulse he describes as the extent of the disturbance of other impulses in the individual's activities which the thwarting of the impulse involves.[28]

Impulse is defined as a mental event beginning in a stimulus and ending in an act. The stimulus is not, however, an alien intruder, worming its way through us as through a piece of cheese, emerging at the other end as act. Stimuli are only received if they serve some need of the organism, and the form which the response takes depends only in part on the nature of the stimulus, and much more upon the organism's wants.[29]

Happiness is the satisfaction of impulses.[30] The most valuable states of mind are those which involve the widest and most comprehensive coördination of activities, and the least curtailment, con-

27. Pp. 117–123. 28. *Principles of Literary Criticism*, pp. 48, 51.
29. Pp. 86, 87. 30. P. 54.

flict, starvation and restriction. Value is organization. Good is efficiency. The best life is one in which as much of a man as possible is engaged, in which as many of his impulses as possible receive satisfaction.[31]

"It is not the intensity of the conscious experience, its thrill, its pleasure, or its poignancy, which gives it value," he says, "but the organization of its impulses for freedom and fullness of life." [32]

We have concerned ourselves, briefly, with the views of Holt, Joad, and Richards, for the reason that they make explicit the basis of the coherence theory, and thus make criticism possible. As we have said, the theory is asserted by Alexander, but not argued; and with a bare assertion there is nothing one can do, except listen to it. We are now in position to consider the theory critically, and to such a consideration we now turn.

IV. IS COHERENCE GOODNESS?

As we have stated, the coherence theory may take one of two forms, depending on the nature of the coherence we mean. It may be (1) the coherence of the individual whose impulses cohere with one another; or (2) the coherence of an individual whose will coheres with the wills of his fellows, or the coherence of a society which allows a maximization of coherence within each individual by offering the conditions which make that possible.

It is not possible to merge these forms of the theory and treat them together without falling into confusion. If Alexander had not frozen them into one indeterminate mass, our task would be lighter and his doctrine would be tangible and ponderable. We shall, therefore, need to treat of each of the forms in turn.[33]

A. What Mr. T. S. Eliot, in his review of Richards' *Science and Poetry*, said of that author's doctrine, is true of all who maintain the first form of the coherence theory; namely, that it presents a psychological theory of value, but not a moral one.[34]

31. P. 59, *Vide* also, by the same author, *Science and Poetry*.
32. *Principles of Literary Criticism*, p. 132.
33. Alexander, as we have indicated, would probably reject the first formulation, if he were pressed to make a choice. We shall, however, treat of it, as the point of view is a significant one, and is, as we have seen, not an unpopular one.
34. In the *Dial* for April 1927, pp. 239–241.

We might agree, says Mr. Eliot, that the goal of the individual is the avoidance of conflict and the attainment of an equilibrium. But just how much help is that to us when we are concerned with the moral problem? Is there any sense in saying, e.g., that St. Francis might have chosen a life in which *more* of his impulses would have been engaged—a life in which an impulse towards fine clothes, say, might have been included?

This introduces us to a multitude of difficulties the theory presents, but the leading one has been stated by Plato in the *Gorgias*,[35] where, in the battle of nature and law dramatically waged between Socrates and the Sophists, Socrates tells Callicles that those desires only which improve a man's character by their gratification, and not those which deteriorate it, should be fulfilled.

For one thing, the ideal of the integrated individual is *impossible* of achievement; though its proponents profess to be maintaining a *Realethik!*

My western conscience, [wrote Amiel in his Journal,] [36] soaked in Christian moralism, has always persecuted my Oriental quietism. Between the relative that overwhelms me, and the absolute I despair of attaining, I hover heedlessly, and I act only at the last extremity. Before any optional action, I doubt; before any speculative decision, I hesitate. I have not dared to be a thorough Buddhist. I am neither an Oriental nor a Westerner, neither a man nor altogether a woman; I have remained amorphous, atomic, agamous, neutral, lukewarm, and divided.

It is only in a rare imaginative experience, when the mind breaks its bounds, and leaps with the swiftness and bravery that are unmatched by things known to our senses, that a man can feel that his internal dialectic has achieved a synthesis, that today, as Flaubert wrote to a correspondent,[37] he is "man and woman together, lover and mistress at once." It is only in such a rare moment that one can sing, with Ruckert, after Rumi, that

I am the mast, the rudder, the steersman and the bark,
I am intoxication, the wine press, the grapes and the wine,
I am the tippler, the inn and the goblet crystalline,

35. *Gorgias*, 503.   36. II, 74.   37. *Correspondence*, II, 232.

The candle and what circles round it, the night-blooming butterfly frail,
The rose and, made drunk by the red rose, the amorous nightingale.

On the contrary, living constantly presents a conflict of two equally impelling and, considered a-morally, equally justifiable desires, which the facts of existence make incompatible. Such conflicts contain the essence of the tragic, for without the sacrifice of one, there is no solution. Man's imagination is boundless, his sympathies without limit, knowing no difference in clime, age, race, and the essence of sympathy and imagination is identification of the self with the not-self: "*du gleichst dem Geist den du begreifst,*" said Goethe; but clime, age, race, and the other conditions of existence which we find but do not make, teach us constantly that infinite spirit is bound by finite body, confined by it, and it cannot be all things to every thing. Man is constantly making choices, and the choice of one thing means the suppression of another, and in the end more lives are buried with him than he has lived.

Then, too, there are some interests which claim, not a part in a whole, but the whole of life. Love is such a thing—

> *All thoughts, all passions, all delights,*
> *Whatever stirs this mortal frame,*
> *All are but ministers of love,*
> *All feed his sacred flame;*

pleasure, another; justice; patriotism; art; God. Integration, coherence, on such terms, means only infinite reincarnation, an eternity of time in which one can live through the various roles of soldier, mystic, lover, adventurer, and what not! [38]

38. "Death is not a haven of rest. It is a starting-point for fresh labors. But if the trials are great, so is the recompense. We miss much here by our own folly, much by unfavorable circumstances. Above all, we miss much because so many good things are incompatible. We cannot spend our youth both in the study and in the saddle. We cannot gain the benefit both of unbroken health and of bodily weakness, both of riches and of poverty, both of comradeship and of isolation, both of defiance and of obedience. We cannot learn the lessons alike of Galahad and of Tristram and of Caradoc. And yet they are all so good to learn. Would it not be worth much to be able to hope that what we missed in one life might come to us in another?" McTaggart, *Some Dogmas of Religion*, p. 138.

Many of us, perhaps each of us at some time or other, prefer one glorious moment to a year of "coherent" living; a moment—despite Mr. Richards—whose intensity, poignancy, or ecstasy—like that of the male bee on his nuptial flight—is ample compensation for a lifetime of drudgery, and "fullness" of sober, pedestrian existence.[39]

And the value of such an experience is that it comes only for a moment; that it is an oasis in a lifetime's desert. Tanner says, in *Man and Superman*, "Yes, a lifetime of happiness! If it were only the first half-hour's happiness, I would buy it for you with my last penny. But a lifetime of happiness! No man alive could bear it: it would be hell on earth."

We have, of course, heard of people who are reputed to have lived a balanced life and were then gathered to their fathers. Our suspicion is that their "much-vaunted balance of personality," as Meier-Graefe has said of Van Gogh's father, "was the result merely of lack of sympathy."

In brief, the difficulties we find with the first form of the coherence theory are: (1) That is is a psychological, not a moral, theory of value. The coherence of a rogue may make him a good rogue, but not a good man. (2) That what may make a man great in our estimation is not his coherence (which probably is his lack of imagination), but his conflicts; that he is a battlefield, so to speak, on which armies, which cannot live in peace together, fight for supremacy. And (3) that the value of coherence may be that it presents a framework for living through a moment whose worth is only its intensity, its ecstasy. This proposition is an echo of Unamuno's cry "for heat, not light!"

B.(1) The other form of the theory presents similarly heavy difficulties. It offers, in the first place, no moral test; for a society, no less than an individual, may be bad and coherent. For example, exclude the Jews, Communists, Socialists and pacifists from Hitlerite Germany, and Nazi Germany will be an example *par excel-*

39. A Greek legend tells how the mother of Achilles put before him the choice between a long life, or a short life full of deeds and struggles, and how he chose the latter.

lence of a coherent state—but its coherence will have been attained by oppression and militarism; and its cohering wills will be those of individuals condemned in the moral judgment of the world. The point is quite obvious: Coherence may be a character of the moral society, but it is not the test of its morality.

The retort might, conceivably, be made that the example is unfairly chosen; for the theory means not the coherence of Hitlerite wills, but of fully-living, freely-developing individuals. But the theory has, as its essential character, this qualification: that in the good society the individual's freedom to live his life is determined and defined by his neighbor's will; and in Nazi Germany it was Hitler and Goebbels who defined the pleasure of that will, who said that only thus and thus can we look upon your will as being in harmony with the *Geist* of the renascent Reich. To this, we think, the proponent of the theory can make no reply, and if he were a German, he could either bide by his "station and its duties" or accept exile or death. For the ideal of the new Prussian State was coherence—one land, one language, one people, one mind.

Professor Hocking, in his book on *The Spirit of World Politics*, suggests three measures of the backwardness of peoples, such as mandated and colonial peoples; namely, (1) mastery of nature—science and its applications, economic and military; (2) public morality, and (3) the condition of the common people.[40] We need not accept these tests; but we always do judge peoples as being backward or progressive, and the judgment is not merely political, in a strict sense, but also moral. Such judgment is unavoidable in the interplay of human relations, and the coherence of the society we judge is barely considered; perhaps for the reason that no community or nation (or individual, for that matter) is without the character of, at least, a formal harmony of its diverse elements, else we would not speak of it as a society. Coherence is the *sine qua non* of public morality; but not its definitive character or essence.

(2) The theory contemplates liberty in the individual which is consonant with equal liberty in everyone else. It is the ideal proposed by Heraclitus, and echoed and re-echoed since his day by

40. Ch. II.

political thinkers, "To combine that degree of liberty without
which law is tyranny, with that degree of law without which
liberty becomes license." But what the protagonists of the coherence theory overlook is that the law which delimits the individual's liberty is, as often as not, the expression, in legislation, of a
moral belief, which says, in effect, that one has the liberty to do that
only which is good, just, and honest. The individual's liberty in
society is only to do those things which society permits him. It is
only at seventy, as Confucius said, that a man may do what his
heart desires without transgressing what is right. A man coheres
with his group by accepting and bearing the yoke of the law and
morals. He does not, on reaching his majority, call his fellows to
him and say to them, Let us now enter into a social compact which
will define, for a time at least, my rights over you and my duties
towards you. That is to say, his coherence does not create goodness. *There is the conception of goodness which defines the terms
of coherence for the individual.*

In effect, the precedence of the moral law over the formal character of organization is recognized by those who maintain the coherence theory; for, as we have said, the foundation of the theory
is the belief that politics and morals should be based on the conception of the good as the satisfaction of impulse or desire. This is
implied, indeed, in even our quotation from Heraclitus. Professor
Hobhouse has, in effect, expanded the thought and made explicit
its end:

> There is no true opposition between liberty as such and control
> as such, for every liberty rests on a corresponding act of con-
> trol. The true opposition is between *the control that cramps the
> personal life and the spiritual order* and the control that is aimed
> at securing the external and material conditions of their free and
> unimpeded development.[41]

But this, as we have pointed out, is instinct with insuperable
difficulties. For what is this personal life and spiritual order? It is
not the liberty to appease each impulse, nor even to order into
coherence as many of men's impulses as one can; for it is inevitable

41. *Liberalism*, p. 147. Italics supplied.

that we judge our impulses by a moral law. And the spiritual order—would Professor Hobhouse have done obeisance to the spiritual order of a modern Fascist state?

From whatever point we view the matter, we are driven to the same conclusion: the coherence theory supplies no moral guide, nor even defines the limits of political activity. For its norms are as easily satisfied by the Kingdom of Hitler as by the Kingdom of Heaven.

V. ULTIMATE ISSUES

If we are not to give up coherence entirely, but attempt to retain it as far as is possible, consonant with our criticisms of the theory, what remains of it? Only this: That while coherence may not be the essence of goodness, there is no goodness where coherence is absent. For the good must, at least, fit into a system, *belong*. It cannot be an Ishmaelite quality, so to speak, having its hand against everybody and everything. It may not be coherent with the present character of its environing circumstances; it may, like the prophet's voice, exist to condemn the organization of which it is a part; but if it is *good* character or conduct, it is good in some larger or other systematic whole of which it is a functioning part, a system projected in contemplation, an "ideal," some Promised Land. Adapting a passage from Kant, the test of the good conduct or character does not lie in its actual approbation, in the actual consent of individuals. It is just if it is consistent with the principle of Right and may secure the possible consent, though temporarily consent is actually withheld.[42]

A moral judgment, then, involves two notions: that of the Right or the Good, and that of the systematic nature of moral values or goods.

Let it be clear that we are not contemplating the first form of the coherence theory. To try to eke anything from it would be like milking a he-goat. For it cannot be maintained that the system of reference is the isolated individual; because, as we have shown, it is not possible to make his impulses cohere; because, he may always throw "discretion" to the winds and prefer the ecstasy of one

42. *Principles of Political Right*, Hastie transl. p. 47.

crazy moment to a lifetime of sobriety; because, though he attain coherence, you may still ask, Is he good?—for the roses and raptures of "vice" may cohere with one another no less than the lilies and languors of "virtue."

Besides, the life of the isolated individual is an abstraction. One cannot seriously ask himself the question what he might do if he were alone. He is *not* alone. Nature tells him so. His experiences tell him so. Indeed, even those desires the satisfaction of which seems to him to be of a most intimate nature, are part of his social heritage. The character of his love, e.g., is set for him by the literature, music, economics, and social institutions of his generation—by the movies, the radio, style in dress, marriage, birth-control and divorce laws, his ability to earn a livelihood in his community, etc. You cannot consider him as though he were enclosed within the walls of his flesh; certainly not judge him thus. A moral judgment of the individual is, at the same time, a judgment of the institutions he maintains or against which he revolts. He may have created them; *but they recreate him.* And, of course, *alone* he could not have created them at all. They express the way in which his separate wants became transmuted into common wants. They are the result of the method by which his satisfactions became possible only through the satisfactions of his neighbors' wants. Self-interest is ineradicable. But enlightened self-interest discovers, soon enough, that to endure, it must become permeated by broader interests, that its private ends must not become anti-social.

De Gourmont has said that an individual can develop himself more conveniently by immorality than by morality. For morality is determined to preserve the race at the expense of the individual.

That is like saying that something may be good for the hive but not for the bees. The hive is a community of individuals; nothing more. It would be non-existent without them; and the individual would perish outside of it. To look upon man apart from his community and upon society apart from its constituents, is to indulge in two abstractions—precisely what De Gourmont did.

The individual may revolt against the morality of his time and place; but he can do so only in the name of a higher or better morality. "For to be no part of any body," as Donne says in a letter, "is to be nothing." A Marxist may counsel a taking up of arms to shatter the national organization of which he is a member; but, if he has our audience, it is because he does not preach violation of the moral law. It is because he cries that our moral system, judged by an enlightened moral sense, is found wanting—is *im*-moral. The appeal is not from one abstraction (a beeless hive) to another (a hiveless bee), but from one moral system to another.

The good, then, is always in terms of social organization. Its meaning is systematic. Plato was perhaps the first to demonstrate this truth. What is justice? he asks at the outset in the *Republic*. But he offers no answer until he has first constructed his state. Justice, he then said, is doing your function and exercising your special virtue in a society whose organization you think is a realization of the moral end of man.

From this point of view, it may be said that, given the system, the just is as objective as the true, and it is not then a question of will or motives. It is only the character of the *act* that is judged, and the individual only as *agent*. The member of society either does, or fails to do, what the system requires of him; and the act either does or does not fit into the order of things. Both are judged in the same way. For the object that is the consequent of the act, considered morally, does not exist apart from the order of moral objects; and when the agent is judged in relation to his act, it is not the act in isolation that is considered, but in its place in the system. Thus, e.g., it may be good to build a hospital if the community is in need of one; but it is waste and misapplied sympathy if there are already a sufficient number of hospitals. But supposing the community needs a hospital, and John Doe builds one, not out of charity, but out of vainglory; the institution is equally good, and John Doe, regardless of his motive, is a good agent. He is judged in the same way that the object is judged—pertinence to the system. The will is viewed as a thing that does or does not fit in the organization. The manufacture of dynamite, say, is prohibited in a society intent upon realizing peace at all costs. In such a system the judgment of the bellicose individual will be no different from that of a stick of dynamite; and there will be no thought of punishment or retribution, but only of making the will fit into the system—like repairing a machine,—or eliminating it—like scrapping a machine. In the system, the good is absolute, for the end is fixed, and anything—man, beast, machine, or institution—either is or is not instrumental in the achievement of that end—the maintenance and perpetuation of the good society.

The good society? But what is the good society? This question marks the last infirmity of an inquiring mind. The Good is indefinable; perhaps unknowable. Postulate a social state, like the Platonic, and it is fairly easy to determine if a particular course of conduct therein is good or bad. But how will it be determined that the Platonic state is good? Will one who believes that society should be classless consider the Republic the ideal community? And how will one judge between Plato and Marx?

This is as far as we can go in the analysis of the moral problem: and the result is a clash of systems, strife among ideals. And it is this which makes the human scene so passionately interesting, and human endeavor so devastatingly tragic; that makes of puny man a majestic god, and the life of the gods a poignant irony.

CHAPTER 7

Truth

I. REALITY AND TRUTH

*A*LL OF THE tertiary qualities are characters of the subject-object relation; but they are differently determined. Goodness is determined by the subject, limited by conditions imposed by external environment; in beauty, the connection between subject and object is more intimate and inseparable; but the character of truth is determined by the object, though truth is a property of judgment.

Art is significant because of mind's imputations; the meaning of a work of art is imported into it; it is mind-saturated. Goodness is an affair of motives or will, and external nature is material only in so far as it is that in respect of which we realize our moral nature. In both cases, the value seems to be "projected" by the subject; it is the "impression" the mind makes on the material world, leaving it beautiful or good.

In the truth situation, Alexander maintains, our personal presence is necessary, but our imputations must be left out. As Bacon says, "Nature is only conquered by obedience." Personality does not control; the object does. Subject is only spectator. Science is pure discovery; not creation. Truth is reality as possessed by mind. Truth differs from reality in that it is possessed by mind, though the mind does not color the object, and is not only impersonalized but depersonalized.

Truth is a value because, like goodness and beauty, it satisfies a human impulse. In the case of truth, the impulse is intellectual curiosity. It is also a value because, like art, it selects departments of the world, and creates a body of its conclusions by arguments of its own, governed by its own convenience, following logical laws, "though these in the end are only broad outlines in things and not pure human inventions." [1] Its entities, e.g., mathematical symbols, have a will of their own, like a novelist's characters. "In its greatest liberty of abstraction, and following out its own abstractions, it is unconsciously turning its eyes towards imprisonment in particulars again." [2] There are no such things, for truth, as pure mental creations; the validity of even quasi-artistic mathematical objects is not derived from mind alone; mathematics is true of the world because its subject is abstracted from the world of things and never loses its connection therewith. In truth, symbols are verified by the actual facts of experience; science is experimental and the symbols express the metric properties of the world of things. Measurement is our work, but the world is measurable and its units are standards. Science describes, organizes, structuralizes the world, and is verified by the organization and structure in the world.

Truth, though a human invention, is impersonal. Its materials are the natural facts and events which are real but not true. Truths are about facts, and are mental constructions. That the rose, e.g., is red, is a fact.

But when I say it is true that this rose is red, I mean that my belief agrees with other beliefs of other men who see the rose, and with all the other beliefs I or others have about the habits of roses. . . . Error consists, therefore, of judgments or beliefs which will not fit in with the judgments of other men about this or other connected topics, or even with other judgments of my own. [3]

The scientist does not interfere with reality as the artist does. He is led by reality. "He uses himself in order in the end to leave himself out." [4] Science is like art, however, in these respects: it is a pos-

1. "Art and Science," 1 *Jour. Phil. St.* 5, at p. 16.
2. *Ibid.*, p. 18.
3. "The Artistry of Truth," 23 *Hibbert Jour.* 294. Cf. *Space, Time, and Deity*, II, pp. 257 ff.
4. "The Artistry of Truth," loc. cit.

session of the mind, an amalgamation of reality with the mind; and, also, it depends on selection and manipulation of its materials by the mind; and, finally, it is expressive, "only whereas art is expressive of the soul of the artist, or the spectator, truth is expressive of the reality which it portrays." [5]

"When we group animals or plants that we have observed singly, it is we who bring the individuals into classes, and we are intervening in nature, though still not interfering." [6]

Inference is artistry, for nature acts and does not infer. Yet, "the laws we establish by inference are the ways of nature's own behaviour, not figments of our mind, not mere ideas which we use, but intimate plans or structures of the world of things and events." [7]

History is dependent on mind for establishing the facts, and collating ideas; thus it is like science, a free movement of mind in grouping significantly, and the mind's process is restricted by the facts. So, too, biology, chemistry, physics.

The more science advances, the more abstract does it become and the more does the mind intervene by its hypotheses and coördinating notions; but the mind is instrumental rather than constitutive. We argue from signs rather than causes; from alternatives or probabilities; yet reasons are founded on causes, and things do admit of being arranged into classes which exclude each other.

Still, the truth, however closely it responds to reality, is not reality. Physics is more obviously an art than other sciences, for physical objects become metrical constructions; the objects of physics are groups of metrical characters which are not perceptual objects but only symbolic of them. Yet the "pointer-readings" are purely symbolic of percepta and not merely an abstraction from that object of its metrical characters. The mind takes from nature what is already in nature.

Alexander criticizes Eddington's idealism, especially the notion that physics is completely an art, conforming to forms of structure chosen by mind. "Mind may act wilfully in ordering its physical world," says Alexander, "but if it does so according to ideas, those

5. *Ibid.*   6. *Ibid.*
7. "Theism and Pantheism," 25 *Hibbert Jour.* 251–2.

ideas seem themselves to have come from physical experience, and to be in the end empirical or experimental notions suggested by external experience, and by the self as the most familiar instance of that experience." [8] Ideas are not creations of mind but abstractions of the most general aspects of concrete experience. Kronecker is right that even the integers of pure mathematics are God-made and not man-made. "We find in nature the forms of our choosing," says Alexander, "because we have chosen them after first finding them in nature." [9] Thus, universals are an item in the world itself. And relativity means that the world is such that from whatever point of view we split space-time in our measurements so as to get different actual measurements, the laws of physics remain the same for all observers or for every point of view. There is no discontinuity between perceptions and thoughts; thought comes from the selection of certain aspects of perceptual matter;—mind may go beyond perception, but it will not create new material, but only combine its store of materials in ways to suit its own purposes. The material of mind is only borrowed from external nature and is not mind's own creation.

Calculus seems to be an example of creation unqualifiedly the mind's own, for therein the mind follows in elaboration its own laws of implication and inference; but even here there is coherence with the basal elements given in whole numbers and created by God and not man. It seems to take us far away from integers, yet never does it lose touch of them completely—even when the integer is treated as a class of classes. "For though a class is a mental conception, and there are no classes in actual reality, yet reality does contain individuals which, though not mental, suffer themselves to be so grouped because they possess the same qualities." [10]

II. WHAT MAKES TRUTH TRUE?

A.

"There is one mode of answering this question to which we are compelled by the whole spirit of our enquiry to give short shrift.

8. 5 *Jour. Phil. St.* 331, at p. 345.   9. *Ibid.*
10. *Ibid.*

It is the so-called correspondence theory of truth: a proposition is true if it agrees with reality, false or erroneous if it does not." [11]

Alexander rejects the correspondence theory, for how, he asks, "shall we know reality and bring our beliefs to that test, except in the form of other propositions? If the reality is something other than what appears to us 'by all the ways' of sense, ideas, imagination, memory, conception, judging, it cannot be appealed to." [12]

Not correspondence to reality makes truth true, but coherence. Truth in any subject-matter depends on whether or not the reality about which the proposition is conversant admits or excludes the proposition in virtue of the occupation by the reality in question of a particular configuration in Space-Time, and the truth is determined by collective judging. True propositions cohere with reality, false propositions are rejected by it. The rejection is performed at the guidance of reality through a clash of minds. "For the reality itself cannot be said to exhibit incoherence, since all occupation of Space-Time is orderly." [13]

True propositions are those which settle down into a system with one another; errors are propositions which do not cohere with the rest and are discarded. And a proposition is incoherent with other propositions about that reality in so far as the occupation by the reality in question of a particular configuration in Space-Time is different from the features contained in the erroneous propositions; "and this is discovered by experiment." [14] "Physically, the thing judged is in a certain respect different from the property imputed to it in the erroneous judging." [15] Alexander illustrates his meaning by the following example. Take the erroneous belief that an animal can live without oxygen. Experiment shows that the animal dies in an atmosphere without oxygen. Therefore, the proposition which declares that an animal dies under such conditions is true, and, since life necessitates the presence of oxygen, the proposition stated at first is erroneous and incoherent with the true proposition. It is in this sense that the coherent propositions which make up a given department of reality are incoherent with errors.

11. *Space, Time, and Deity*, II, 252.   12. *Ibid.*
13. *Ibid.*, II, 253.   14. *Ibid.*, II, 255.   15. *Ibid.*

The incoherence of the error with the truth does not lie in the conflict of the true believing with the erroneous believing. The conflict exists between the beliefs,

> but it follows and is parallel to the contemplated incoherence. For in cognition we watch and do not make. Our believings are guided by the reality outside us, and we do not make the reality but find it. It is only the *truth* that we make when we compare ourselves with one another.[16]

The distinction between the coherence of certain propositions with one another and their incoherence with others is determined by reality itself. But the distinction comes into existence only through the conflict and coöperation of many minds, and the propositions are true only in their relation to the minds which have reality for their possession and reject the judgments of the erroneous minds. Thus, truth is a creation of mind at the bidding of reality. It implies a relation not to individual as individual, but to the individual mind in its attitude to the social mind, that is to the individual as a standard mind.

> The mind which has truth has it so far as various minds collectively contribute their part to the whole system of true beliefs; the mind which has error is so far an outcast from the intellectual community. Thus while on its objective or contemplated side, error is detected by being convicted of introducing an element of reality which does not belong to the reality investigated, on its subjective or believing side it fails to cohere with social believings.[17]

Truth means the settling down of individual beliefs into a social whole and the condemnation of the heretical or unscientific believing.

B.

It appears, from our foregoing exposition, that there are for Alexander two tests of truth, parallel and coextensive. *On the objective side,* as he says, truth consists in asserting of reality an

16. *Ibid.,* II, 257. Italics in text.   17. *Ibid.,* II, 258.

element which belongs to it; *on the subjective side*, truth consists in believing what the "social mind" believes. And somehow or other the two are always parallel; i.e., a truth on the subjective side will always have a truth on the objective side and not an error or falsehood.

Let us consider, first, truth on the subjective side. The objection occurs readily to mind that mayhap the mind which has *truth* is an outcast from the intellectual community, e.g., Bruno, Galileo. "One is ten thousand to me if he be the best," says Heraclitus, and so it must be to everyone. The memorial statue to Bruno was put up by the generation that he foresaw and not by the generation into which he was born.

Alexander lays himself readily open to such easy refutation because he fails to distinguish various types of objects of knowledge, which result in corresponding types of scientific laws. (1) The simplest kind of laws describe the relations of *sense objects*, and go to make up the theory of *perceptual objects*. (2) The second kind is that concerned with the relations of perceptual objects, and these are causal laws. (3) Finally there are the laws relating to scientific objects, the theories of modern science.[18]

Now Alexander's test "on the subjective side" may hold for the first type of law, but not for the latter two. Regarding the first, some sense objects are, e.g., the so-called secondary qualities. For Alexander, they are altogether objective. But it is known that some people are, e.g., color-blind; i.e., their experience with colors is not that of the "normal" man. But they do not disprove the objectivity of colors. They suffer from a visual defect. A color of a thing is what the generality of mankind agree on. This expedient of Alexander's—i.e., the social test of truth—is easily understandable when we have regard only to sense-objects; for how else could he assert unqualified objectivity? Thus, "the agreement of many persons in the belief that the rose is yellow and not white does not make the rose really yellow, it only follows that reality." [19] It is clear that what he maintains is that the collective nose, so to speak, will never follow a *false* scent; and it is also clear why he does

18. Cf. Ritchie, *Scientific Method*, Ch. VI.
19. *Space, Time, and Deity*, II, 254.

maintain this, for after all it saves sense-objects from subjectivity.[20]

But it is only in the elementary classificatory stage of science that the laws describing the relations of sense objects are found. Science is in the main concerned with more complex types of laws that describe relations between perceptual bodies rather than between sensible qualities, and with the still more complex and general types, as, e.g., the kinetic theory, the laws of thermodynamics, the Copernican theory and the theory of relativity. What the collective mind has to do with these types of law it is not easy to see. The validity of the theory of evolution is not dependent on the suffrage of the people of Tennessee; nor the truth or falsity of the psychoanalytic explanation of the causes of insanity on agreement among alienists.

Turning now to the test of truth "on the objective side," Alexander's view is full of ambiguities. On the one hand, he says that the test is systematic coherence; on the other, that it is correspondence of proposition with reality.

There is good reason for this absence of definitiveness, which reason we shall attempt to present. Coherence is itself a character of Reality, "since all occupation of Space-Time is orderly." [21] "For nothing in our experience . . . is isolated and stands absolutely by itself, but is apprehended with its surrounding fringe of Space-Time." [22] He defines belief as the awareness that what is judged belongs to Space-Time as a whole, and he agrees with Bradley that every judgment is ultimately about the whole Reality.[23] "*Die Wahrheit ist das Ganze.*"

It appears, then, that coherence is founded in reality itself (though selection is *also* the result of mind). Science in no sense submits "the shows of things to the desires of the mind." Cognition is a direct revelation of reality, and reality has the character of coherence. Reality is a whole for Alexander no less than for the absolute idealist; only it is not a whole that centers in mind. For both, knowledge has the double nature of continuity of mind and reality, only for the former the universe is without consciousness

20. We only mean that this may be the motive for Alexander's adoption of the social test, not that it will justify the adoption. It is a gloss on the text.
21. *Ibid.*, II, 253.   22. *Ibid.*, II, 247.   23. *Ibid.*, II, 248.

at its center. The absolute idealist may, therefore, speak of coherence and not of correspondence as the test of truth, for the systematic unity of reality is, to him, an attribution of mind,[24] and
"there is no true whole but mind." [25]

But not so for Alexander. Coherence is a character of Space-
Time itself. *It is a test of truth because it is a character of reality.*
But it is not *really* the test. *The test is the correspondence of coherence among propositions with the coherence among configurations of Space-Time;* not the correspondence of a sensation with
a sensum,—for, as we have seen, there is no "pure" sensation *and
all knowledge is systematic,*—but the correspondence of systems
of ideas with systems of "bits" of Space-Time.

If Alexander's universe of Space-Time were not a continuum, if
each finite space were not part of a wider one,[26] he could maintain
the correspondence theory simply. Thus Mr. Russell's world consisting of events which are short, small and haphazard, a world
without unity and continuity,[27] necessitates the correspondence
test.[28] So, too, does a universe like Mr. Ritchie's, which allows of
"disorder." [29]

And if any universe is orderly, it is Alexander's. And if any order
is independent of mind, it is that of Space-Time. There are no
mental categories that need to grind the grist of reality or supply
a medium of cohesion. Even universals are independent of mind.
There is nothing for mind to do but correctly register the scene
on its photographic plate. Alexander cannot, therefore, accept
the coherence theory simply.

His whole line of argument leads to only one possible resolution;
namely, that the test of truth is correspondence of coherences,
the correspondence of mental system to physical system, of ideal
whole or coherence to real whole or coherence; neither simple
coherence nor simple correspondence, but correspondence of
coherences.

24. Vide, e.g., Bosanquet, *Distinction Between Mind and Its Objects,*
Appendix.
25. Bosanquet, *Philosophical Theory of the State,* 43.
26. *Space, Time, and Deity,* I, 42.   27. *The Scientific Outlook,* 98.
28. *Our Knowledge of the External World,* 40–63.
29. *Scientific Method,* 200.

This is, we believe, the meaning of Alexander, though, admittedly, it is a far jump from what he says. How, otherwise, can his theory be freed from confusion and self-contradiction? Had he apprehended the elements of his theory with more clarity, he would not have been led, too, to adopt the view that truth is a character of belief or judgment. At nearly every point of his theory of truth Alexander comes pretty close to giving up the ghost of realism. A much simpler line of thought for him would be to hold that since coherence or system is a character of meaning, and reality itself is systematic, truth is correspondence of symbol and referent, when the symbol is considered not arbitrary but natural, and its meaning is, therefore, metaphysical and not merely logical. Truth would be a property of some meaning situations; those situations, namely, where the symbol is taken to have a metaphysical transcendence and stands, in fact, for an existent. The test of the truth of a belief would be not by belief, but by meaning, or the correspondence of the existence of symbol with the existence of referent.

Meaning itself does not imply the existence of the referent, or the terminus in an object, but only the direction of objectivity. It is an activity, and it is expressed by an intention or supposal no less than by a dogmatic judgment. What is meant is never the content or symbol itself. Meaning is wider than existence; and what is important for it is objective reference and not objective existence. Truth is irrelevant to a meaning situation unless the reference is to a metaphysical object, and then its test is the existence of that object.

Coherence, then, is not a test of truth; but, since meaning is wider than existence, we may construct systems of meanings with no reference to objective existence, and the propositions within the system will then have coherence as their test—but not of *truth*, only of their *validity*, or *deontological truth*. Not the laws of existence, but of logic, will be the standard. To make what is the test of such artificial or postulated systems, the test also of metaphysical truth, is altogether without warrant, and is probably the result, directly or indirectly, of an inadequate or false analysis of the types of meaning situations.

"The mind of man seems to be of a nature to assimilate itself to the universe; we belong to the world; the world is mirrored in us. Therefore, when we bend our thoughts on a limited object, we concentrate faculties which are naturally endowed with infinite correspondences." [30]

30. Christopher Dawson, *The Age of the Gods.*

*W*e have seen that art is to be understood only through an analysis of meaning. Only by the results of such an analysis is the impasse reached between the formalists and programmists capable of being bridged. The aesthetic situation involves a bidirectional meaning transaction, for the work of art is *meant* and *means*, and criticism should be based on an appreciation of the entire situation, neither direction nor terminus taking precedence over the other or considered apart from the other. Further, we have seen, in a work of art, as in an object of knowledge generally, there is to be found the fusion or amalgam of percept and concept; or, stating it otherwise, a work of art *means* in a double sense; namely, it means systematically and it means intensionally.

Alexander's aesthetic theory, on the contrary, is exclusively in terms of the individual coherence or form of the work of art—the coherence of part with part, some elements in the thing itself and some supplied by mind. The theory is a paradox from beginning to end. Mind imputes characters or elements or "parts" to the object, yet the object as a work of art is free from conceptual data and is not at all representative. Each part, mental or physical, coheres with the other parts, and so has a meaning, but the object as an organic unit means nothing but itself. It is appreciated in its meaningless "purity."

We do not presume to think that our doctrine exhausts the possibilities of a philosophy of art. It is not even a Prolegomena to All Future Aesthetics. We do submit, however, that the view offers possibilities; and it may be that an analysis of meaning, more thoroughgoing than we have been able to supply, will help exhaust the subject of aesthetics.

The analysis of meaning as related to a theory of knowledge or truth has resulted in our acceptance of meaning as the key, so to speak, to truth. Our conclusions may be summarized briefly: (1) Meaning is wider than existence. Meaning always has a direction of objectivity, symbol never means itself, but some object, but the object, to be that, need not be an existent, it needs only to be projected. (2) Truth can properly be spoken of only when the objective reference in the meaning situation is to an existent, actual or supposed. In the land of make-believe there is no truth or error. (3) Symbols are arbitrary or natural. Science is concerned with the latter kind. It is interested in necessary connections; necessary connections between the sensible qualities of a perceptible object, or between perceptible objects. The meaning relation is not between arbitrary elements, but between elements standing in a relationship of necessary connection. (4) Truth is the correspondence of symbol and object, symbol being natural and not arbitrary.[1] (5) Symbols may be postulated. When a system of them is constructed, their coherence within the system is their validity, or, if you prefer, their truth (however, in a deontological sense). (6) There are, then, two tests; namely, of truth and of validity; one pertinent in a system of natural symbols or propositions, the other in a system of postulated or arbitrary symbols or propositions. With reference to the former, the test is correspondence; with reference to the latter, the test is coherence or consistency. (7) Alexander accepts the coherence theory of truth. But what he *really* means is that the test is the correspondence of a system of ideas to a system of reals; the correspondence of coherences.

The last point suggests Joachim's discussion of the correspondence theory in *The Nature of Truth*.

> If you have a whole of parts [he says] such that each part contributes determinately to constitute the whole, and that the structural plan of the whole determines precisely the nature of the differences which are its parts, you can compare this whole with another whole of the same type. And you can say "the part x in A (the first whole) corresponds to the part y in B (the second whole).[2]

1. Where we have been speaking of symbol, others would perhaps have used the term content or proposition.　　2. Pp. 9–10.

Correspondence, when attributed to the wholes, means an identity of purpose expressed through materially different constituents as an identical structure or plan; when attributed to the parts, correspondence means identity of function contributed by materially different constituents towards the maintenance of an identical plan or structure.

Taking correspondence in this sense, he concludes that the nature of the structure, or the purpose or idea which it unfolds, emerges more into importance as the essence of truth, while the fact of correspondence shows itself as nothing more than a "symptom" of truth. If, e.g., you say that Euclidean space is the reality correspondence with which constitutes the truth of a judgment, Joachim replies that Euclidean space itself is a system of such judgments, and that the truth of each of them is constituted by its coherence with all the others, but not by its correspondence with anything external to the system.[3]

Now this critique of correspondence has a semblance of force, and, if not questioned, might be taken to substantiate Alexander.[4] But it may be questioned with justice. True, a scientific judgment is tested by coherence with a system of judgments which we call a science. This we have not doubted. But what makes the science true? Alexander can logically give only one possible answer, and that is, correspondence with a system of configurations of Space-Time that are taken as the subject-matter of the particular science. The spirit and logic of his enquiry will permit of no alternative solution. Truth is still "for" mind but not mental.[5]

In our discussion of goodness we came to the conclusion that while an analysis of meaning will carry us a long way, it will not carry us *all* the way. Goodness is always systematic. To be good means to function properly within an organization. The good is thus both absolute and instrumental; it is instrumental in that its meaning is systematic, it is absolute in that its place or function within the system of reference is fixed. So much truth there is, then, in Alexander's position: the good is the coherent.

3. P. 28.
4. That is, the coherence theory as he formulates it, free from correspondence,—not our "restatement."
5. Cf. *Space, Time, and Deity*, II, 253-4.

But further consideration led us to the conclusion that while coherence is a *sine qua non* of goodness, it is not its *differentia*. For a coherent whole may be morally bad.

It might be contended that if an organization is judged to be bad, that does not mean that coherence is not the test of goodness. Two organizations might be subsumed under a wider system, where the thesis and antithesis will find their moral synthesis. Thus, the coherence theory might be said to have a third form.

We are not inclined to accept this resolution. In the first place, the method of subsumption leads ultimately to the all-inclusive universe. And we see no sense in qualifying the whole universe as *good*. If logic will drive us to do this, we must reject that logic as the solution of the moral problem. It may be the *logical* solution, but it is hardly the *moral* solution. Morally we will be left precisely where we were before we started out. For the *fact* is that *all* systems *do* co-exist, and so somehow *do* to an extent cohere in the universe. That is an easy way of rationalizing evil, but is no way of defining the good. Also, the difficulties we found with the second form of the theory are to be found no less with this form. What difference does it make whether the constituents are individual wills or social wills?

When regard is had to the content, and not simply the form, of the contending systems in the world, to speak of a synthesis seems to be a form of temporizing. Social Democrats have been frequently accused of having a too easy disposition to conciliate and compromise, "synthesize"; and their failure to achieve more may be due primarily to this same character. We see no way of having the lamb and the lion lie down together, outside of a messianic era, and expect the lamb to get up ever. The dialectical synthesis in morals and politics is achieved not by subsumption, but by submersion; not by an embrace, but by the ruthless extermination or subordination of the weaker. That is, we believe, the historical fact. Morals may reinterpret history but should not contradict it.

How, then, are systems to be judged? Maybe they cannot be judged. It is even difficult to have the spokesmen for the opposing factions understand one another, let alone reach a determination that will satisfy them both. Probably the preference is ultimately irrational (that is, of course, if one has not a stake in either system). We should not like to think so. Such a view may lead to a moral paralysis; or even, as in the case of the "disvaluers of value," to the brink of despair.

Bosanquet, who also maintains the coherence theory of goodness, says, in passing, that he does not mean to suggest that the action of states is beyond moral criticism. But he offers no standard by which a state could be commended or condemned, and takes refuge in ideals that transcend morality, such as art, philosophy, religion.[6] In this he follows Bradley. No sooner does a man discover what his station is, and its duties, than analysis and enquiry lead him to consider an ideal of social perfection, and then an ideal of non-social perfection.[7] We find in both a frank acceptance of the limitations of the coherence doctrine; an example which, we feel, Alexander might have done well to have followed.

6. *Philosophical Theory of the State,* concluding chapter.
7. *Ethical Studies,* new ed., 225, 244, 279.

Articles, books and lectures by Samuel Alexander, pertinent to the subjects treated in this study, and arranged in chronological order:

ARTICLES

"The Idea of Value," XVII *Mind* (New Series) 31 (1892)
"Natural Piety," XX *Hibbert Journal* 609 (1922)
"The Artistry of Truth," XXIII *Hibbert Journal* 294 (1925)
"Art and Science," I *Journal of Philosophical Studies* 5 (1926)
"Theism and Pantheism," XXV *Hibbert Journal* 251 (1927)
"Lessons from Spinoza," *Chronicon Spinozanum* (1927)
"Morality as an Art," III *Journal of Philosophical Studies* 143 (1928)
"Beauty and Greatness in Art," *Proceedings of the Aristotelian Society* (1929–1930)
"Science and Art," V *Journal of Philosophical Studies* 331 and 516 (1930)
"Truth, Greatness, and Beauty," XXVIII *Hibbert Journal* 616 (1930)
"Poetry and Prose in the Arts," VII *Journal of Philosophical Studies* 15 and 153 (1932)

BOOKS AND LECTURES

Moral Order and Progress; an Analysis of Ethical Conceptions. 1889; 2nd ed. 1891. London: English and Foreign Philosophical Library
The Basis of Realism. 1914. London: Oxford University Press
Space, Time, and Deity. 2 volumes. 1920. London: Macmillan.

Spinoza and Time. Afterword by Viscount Haldane. 1921. London: G. Allen and Unwin, Ltd.

Art and the Material. 1925. Manchester: University Press. London and New York: Longmans, Green and Co.

Art and Instinct. 1927. Oxford: Clarendon Press

Beauty and other Forms of Value. 1933. London: Macmillan.

Philosophical and Literary Pieces. Edited, with memoir, by his literary executor. 1939. London: Macmillan.